Ex Libris:
Charles L. Scheidl

The Rule of Peace

THE RULE OF PEACE

St. Benedict and the European Future

Christopher Derrick

ST. BEDE'S PUBLICATIONS
Still River, Massachusetts

LIBRARY OF CONGRESS CATALOGING IN PUBLICATION DATA

Derrick, Christopher, 1921-
    The rule of peace.

    Bibliography: p.
    1. Benedictus, Saint, Abbot of Monte Cassino. 2. Bene-
dictines — Spiritual life. 3. Europe — Civilization.
4. Civilization, Modern. 5. Civilization, Occidental.
I. Title.
BR1720.B45D47   255'.1   80-20804
ISBN 0-932506-01-1

PREFACE

This book was originally written for the *Association of St. Benedict, Patron of Europe*, and for publication in two or three European languages: its theme is the relevance, for the temporal as well as the spiritual future of that continent, of the values implied in the Rule of St. Benedict and in the life style of his monks.

There is a sense, however, in which "Europe" can be understood as a religious and cultural inheritance and not merely as a geographical expression; and in this wider sense, it seemed possible that my theme might be of some interest to people who share that inheritance in the United States and elsewhere beyond the boundaries of Europe.

I hope that no American reader will take offence if thus invited to consider himself and his future in European terms. No kind of imperialism is intended: the inheritance and the future in question might just as well have been called "Western."

Various passages have been put into quotation marks or indented simply in order to show that they are not my own: this is an essay, not a work of scholarship, and a full *apparatus* of notes and references would have been out of place here. The principal works from which I have quoted, and which I recommend for further reading, are as follows:

Patrick Leigh Fermor, *A Time to Keep Silence*, (London: John Murray, 1957).

Christopher Dawson, *The Making of Europe*, (London: Sheed and Ward, 1932).

Christopher Dawson, *Religion and the Rise of Western Culture*, (London: Sheed and Ward, 1950).

Thomas Merton, *The Silent Life*, (London: Burns and Oates, 1957).

T. F. Lindsay, *The Holy Rule for Laymen*, (London: Burns and Oates, 1947).

E. F. Schumacher, *Small is Beautiful*, (New York: Harper Colophon Books, 1975).

Geoffrey Moorhouse, *Against All Reason*, (London: Weidenfeld and Nicolson, 1969).

St. Benedict's actual *Rule* is, of course, required reading for all—perhaps especially for parents and for all those who hold positions of authority in public or private life.

C. D.

The Rule of Peace

CHAPTER ONE

*T*he great heavy door swings shut behind you, the sound of its latch echoing for a while in this huge dim silence. At once you are in a different world. Such light as there is, filtering down from a high clerestory through Romanesque pillars, seems unlike the light you have just left outside. The silence, when it returns, seems to be something more positive than a mere absence of noise, more charged with some meaning which you cannot yet grasp. Even time seems different. You wait in total stillness for what might be five minutes, or might be eternity, so completely does this atmosphere modify your sense of change and duration.

Then, in the shadowed distance, you see a black-robed figure at work on a rope, so that the faint striking of a clock is followed at once by the slow measured tolling of a great bell overhead. The community enters in solemn procession, bows to the Cross and to its Abbot, forms up in the choir stalls, prays silently, and then—perfectly and at leisure, just as though there was nothing to do except praise the Lord forever—embarks once again on the lucid melodic purity of a slow *Deus in adjutorium meum intende*. The great wheel of monastic worship is turning before you, as it has turned steadily through century upon century of our European past.

The whole of life, as led by these men, forms part of its turning. Soon you will find yourself in the cloister, outside the door of the refectory which the community has entered in silence for its midday meal. As a guest, and therefore a representative of Christ, you will be greeted by the Abbot with the friendliest of smiles and perhaps even with a whispered word or two, and he will make himself your servant, washing your hands according to an old ritual before escorting you to your place at table. The long chanted grace that follows seems like a continuation of what you have just heard in the church; and even when you sit down and begin your lunch (plain peasant food of excellent quality and no pretensions, mostly grown by the monks themselves) it will be in an atmosphere not of relaxation and chatter but of quasi-liturgical silence, broken only by a faint tinkle of cutlery and by the steady voice of the reader, droning on through a chapter of St. Benedict's Rule first of all, and then through some work of theology or piety. The meal will end with another chanted grace, relating it once again to the monks' chief task in life, which is the *Opus Dei* or psalmodic service of God. The act of eating and drinking is woven into an all-pervading texture of worship.

This is true of everything else that the monks do, as you will see if your visit continues, enabling you to watch them in their daily routine and their work, which may involve anything from pig-keeping to high scholarship. You will observe this, and you will also be able to observe these men in themselves, and so formulate an answer to a question which intrigues many people.

What are monks *really* like?

They are ordinary men who have chosen to live—or, according to an old usage, to *fight*—under the Rule of St. Benedict (a short and apothegmatic document composed in sixth-century Italy) and as members of some community which lives by that Rule within the over-riding faith and discipline of the Catholic Church. Contrary to popular myth, they have taken no "vow of silence." The three vows which they do take—only after prolonged preparation, and with full consent on both sides—are of obedience, of stability (which means perseverance in the monastic life and in this particular community), and of *conversio morum* or self-reformation. All this means that they have decided to seek and serve God alone, and to exclude from their lives whatever might separate them from him.

A decision of this kind is very unlike the decisions usually made by young men when hesitating between different careers—so much so that it might almost be called eccentric, even fanatical. Can these men really be called "ordinary"? You study them, perhaps in some curiosity.

One thing becomes clear very soon. Any group of human beings is likely to contain a few eccentrics, a few oddities—the cloister is no exception. But seldom is there any hysteria or fanaticism in its atmosphere. As you observe the monks and get to know them better, as a community and as individuals, you will find that they are indeed "ordinary" in the sense that practically all of them are very normal, very balanced and sane. As human types go, they may well remind you of sailors: they have that kind of cheerful down-to-earth practicality, and their eyes have the characteristic look of those who habitually gaze upon distant horizons.

You will soon discover that there is a recognisable monastic "type" or appearance and manner. Not all monks conform to it, but many do. The face tends to be slightly beaky and bony, though not because of any malnutrition; its skin tends to gleam; the monk's ready smile has a distinctively shy and serious quality to it; he is less accustomed to dealing with strangers than most other men are, and very much more anxious to avoid even the appearance of seeking to dominate his relationships with them. His courtesy is therefore extreme, perhaps a shade effusive; but all the time, you feel that his real attention is elsewhere, upon horizons broader than those watched by sailors. He is glad to be with you, and to help you with your problem of the moment, but he isn't sorry to leave you—a monk talking to a stranger is rather like a fish out of water, and he is happy to get back to his native element.

The waters in which he is most completely at home, most completely himself, are those of the Divine Office, the *Opus Dei*. I have compared this to a great wheel that turns endlessly. It can be compared just as aptly to the timeless surge of an ocean,

> The moving waters at their priestlike task
> Of pure ablution round earth's human shores—

it gives you that same feeling of eternity, of endless change within overall permanence, and it is the monk's home, to which everything else in his life must be related if it is not to become mere interruption.

For most of us, even if we are devoutly practising believers, worship is a kind of exception, an interruption. It is something to which we turn from other and more habitual preoccupations. For the monk, things are the other way round.

The great wheel turns, the great ocean surges; and whatever your personal faith or disbelief, your personal goodness or corruption, it does something to you. From the slow liturgical chant of a great abbey, and from the disciplined life which is its basis and setting and necessary condition, you begin to get a deeper understanding of the single concept and word which is the Benedictine motto: *Pax*, or *Shalom*, or *Peace*.

*   *   *

Peace? Can it ever exist in this world? Our history books and our newspapers suggest not. Can it ever exist in the cloister? And if it can, what relevance does this fact have to your problems and mine? Or to the world's?

What kind of picture have I just painted, anyway? Have the first paragraphs of this book been anything more than a brief exercise in nostalgia and sentimentality, a romantic dream of what monasticism ought to be but seldom is in fact? And if such a monasticism did exist today, should it not be regarded as a monstrous kind of escapism, a refusal to face the full stress and pain of our life in this world and in this century of ecological disaster and vicious human conflict and social breakdown and, all too probably, of final nuclear disaster?

Let me be clear about one thing at least. That brief sketch of the monastic life, as seen by the lay visitor, is not a product of my own romantic imagination. It is a strictly factual description, as objective as I can make it, of my own recent experiences—notably at one particular abbey in France, but at many others too.

But while the picture I have just painted is not idealised, it is slightly generalised. Monasticism varies, in its aesthetics and otherwise. I have mentioned a huge and ancient Romanesque church. Let me now admit that it was once derelict and has been extensively restored, and that the community which serves it is of fairly recent foundation. Any suggestion of unbroken continuity with the Middle Ages and earlier would be deceptive in literal fact, however true in spirit. That great wheel of monastic worship has indeed turned unceasingly since the sixth century, but there are very few places where it has turned without interruption, and this is not one of them.

Nor does it always turn in a place of rich archaic beauty. Many monastic buildings of the present day, though still serving their ancient purpose, are starkly and even aggressively "modern" in design; and in other respects too, a number of present-day communities have started to "modernise" their whole style of life and worship, not always with the happiest consequences. The concept of monasticism is essentially timeless and historically ancient, but it is often embodied in forms which suggest nothing of the kind.

Anyone who wishes to retain his romantic vision of what a monastery is must be very careful about which monastery he visits. Otherwise he may get a nasty shock.

* * *

None the less, that "image" of monasticism as something archaic, rooted deeply and unchangingly in the mediaeval and earlier past of our Western culture, does still correspond with the facts fairly extensively, and it will serve to introduce the theme of this book. My subject is the future of Europe and of European unity, though readers in, say, the United States may interpret this as referring to "the West" in general; and my contention is that if our hopes for this European or Western future are to be realistic, they will need to be based *primarily* upon the wisdom of St. Benedict and the tradition of the monks who have followed him down so many centuries.

This will strike some people as a paradox, even as an absurdity. In the popular imagination, "the monk" exists sometimes as a pathetic figure, sometimes as a grim figure, and sometimes—very often in the pages of such magazines as *Punch* and *The New Yorker*—as a comic figure, a cheery rubicund fellow with a loaf and a cheese and a big flagon of wine and a merry disregard of all those pious rules and regulations. Each of these three images can correspond, here and there, with the facts, but none of them suggests that the monk has anything very serious to say to the modern world. Any closer acquaintance with the monastic institution will make it clear that while monks can be pathetic or grim or comic, most of them are, on the whole, very much like other men. But beyond this, its first effect may well be to confirm the belief that monastic life is so totally unlike any other kind of life as to be irrelevant to anything outside itself.

The apparent totality of this irrelevance may inflict an uncomfortable kind of disorientation upon any layman who visits the cloister, as one English writer discovered.

> Only by living for a while in a monastery can one quite grasp its staggering difference from the ordinary life that we lead. The two ways of life do not share a single attribute; and the thoughts, ambitions, sounds, light, time, and mood that surround the inhabitants of a cloister are not only unlike anything to which one is accustomed, but in some curious way, seem its exact reverse. The period during which normal standards recede and the strange new world becomes reality is slow, and, at first, acutely painful.

This difficulty will be all the greater if the visitor or student does not share the monks' religious background. "To the ordinary secular historian," says Christopher Dawson, "monasticism must remain as alien and incomprehensible a phenomenon as the Lamaism of Tibet or the temple priesthood of the ancient Sumerians. To the Catholic on the other hand, the monastic institution still forms an integral part of his spiritual world." But even he may tend to see it either as something merely picturesque and beautiful, or else as something merely negative and even deathly, and as a kind of escapism above all, a flight from the real problems of this life; and others are very likely indeed to see it in those terms. Milton, for example, was quite sure that the monk was a deserter rather than a brave warrior:

> I cannot praise a fugitive and cloistered virtue, unexercised and unbreathed, that never sallies out and seeks her adversary, but slinks out of the race, where that immortal garland is to be run for, not without dust and heat.

A monk might reply that he never had the purpose of earning Mr. Milton's praise, while gasping at the factual ignorance displayed in those well-known words; and if he was in an uncharitable mood, he might also gasp at the colossal vulgarity displayed by David Hume, no doubt unconsciously, when he addressed the question of whether monasticism is useful or not. "The whole train of monkish virtues," said the philosopher, "...they serve no manner of purpose; neither advance a man's fortune in the world nor render him a more valuable member of society; neither qualify him for entertainment of company nor increase his powers of self-enjoyment." One can agree. If you want to get rich and add to the Gross National Product, if you want to shine among Beautiful People and enjoy yourself generally, don't be a monk. It won't help.

But such replies will only carry weight in friendly ears. The dominant values of our present society are such that if Benedictine monasticism was proposed as some kind of guide and model for the twentieth-century world, and for twentieth-century Europe in particular, most people would respond with scepticism or amusement or contempt. Nothing of that sort (they would say) has the faintest relevance to ourselves and our problems.

But the Popes do not agree. Two of them have recently made just such a recommendation. In 1947, Pius XII declared St. Benedict to be the "Father of Europe," and in the same way but more emphatically, Paul VI declared him to be the "Patron and Protector" of Europe in 1964.

What weight can we attach to such recommendations?

*   *   *

The reader of these pages may not share my own view of the Papacy, or of the weight to be attached to Papal pronouncements on this subject or that. But he may be prepared to admit that the Papacy has been around for a long time, and has gathered much experience and shrewdness of the human kind at least, and is rather exceptionally well placed to see what's happening in the world and to know what can be done about it.

Even so, it may be his instinct to see, in those two declarations of Pius XII and Paul VI, little more than a pious acknowledgement of the great things achieved by Benedictine monasticism in the European past.

It is not in dispute that they *were* great things, and not only by purely spiritual standards. The monks were the civilisers, the makers of Europe. They were the ones who saved what was worth saving from the ruins of the Roman Empire and established the culture of the high Middle Ages, to which we owe most of what we now call "civilisation"—unless we use that word (as some do) to indicate only "barbarism made strong and luxurious by mechanical power." St. Benedict died in 543 A.D., and such was his influence that Newman saw fit to call the next six hundred years "the Benedictine centuries." The so-called Dark Ages, says Christopher Dawson, were above all

> the Age of the Monks, an age which begins with the Fathers of the Desert and closes with the great movements of monastic reform that are associated with the names of Cluny, in the West, and of Mount Athos in the East. The greatest names of the age are the names of monks—St. Benedict and St. Gregory, the two Columbas, Bede and Boniface, Alcuin and Rabanus Maurus, and Dunstan—and it is to the monks that the great cultural achievements of the age are due, whether we look at the preservation of ancient culture, the conversion of the new peoples, or the formation of new centres of culture in Ireland and Northumbria and the Carolingian Empire.

Or, more briefly: "the monastery was the most typical cultural institution throughout the whole period that extends from the decline of classical civilisation to the rise of the European universities in the twelfth century—upwards of seven hundred years."

On purely historical grounds, therefore, we can regard

those two Papal declarations as appropriate. "Benedictine monasticism played such a tremendously important part in the reconstruction of Europe after the great migrations, that Benedict is rightly called not only the Father of Western monasticism but simply 'the Father of the West'."

*   *   *

But is he *only* of interest to historians, and to present-day monks, and to such lay-people—there are quite a number of them—as conduct their private devotional lives in the spirit of his Rule? Let him be called the Father of our Western past; is there any sense in which he can be valued as the Patron and Protector of our Western or European future?

Various positive answers can be offered to such questions; and I want to dismiss two of them very briefly, since they do not form part of my main subject.

In the first place, Catholics have long been in the habit of addressing their prayers not only to God but also to the Saints in Heaven. I take this to be a theologically sound practice and also a form of courtesy and good manners within the Communion of Saints, though it is obviously capable of being misused. (One should not think of Heaven as a kind of worldly court, where it is important to catch the right ear or pull the right string.) From the considerations that follow in this book, it might well be concluded that an individual would do well to make St. Benedict his personal patron, to take his name at Baptism or Confirmation or Religious Profession, to address regular prayers to him. I myself would warmly endorse any such proposal, but I would rather leave this subject to men more spiritual than myself.

Then, in the second place, a papal call to St. Benedict's patronage might be interpreted as a cry for more monks and more abbeys, for a more widespread embracing of the actual monastic vocation. If so, I would gladly make that cry my own, except that, once again, I feel somewhat shy about doing so. In my view, it is a very good thing for society and the Church when a great many people feel called to the monastic life, a very bad thing when such vocations dwindle, and an even worse thing when established communities start to become shaky in monastic discipline and even in the Catholic Faith. (We have seen something of this recently, not for the first time in monastic history.) But if people are to be called to a life of worship and silence and work and obedience and self-abnegation, I am in various ways ill-qualified to do the calling, and would do best to keep my mouth shut about such high matters.

*   *   *

My concern is with a broader understanding, and even a more worldly understanding, of St. Benedict's present-day relevance. The point is that Europe faces a great many problems, and that its future depends crucially on the spirit in which it approaches them. Some of these problems are generally recognised to be religious—or at least moral and spiritual—in nature; others may seem to arise at the human, secular, or pragmatic level alone, though even these will turn out to be religious in the last analysis. Either way, they may now seem incapable of resolution. But there is ample reason, both theoretical and practical, to believe that they would resolve themselves pretty well automatically—in so far as human problems can be resolved at all in this life—if we started to think and behave somewhat more monastically, in something closer to the spirit of St. Benedict.

What I am proposing might be called a specialised application of the general Christian principle that if we seek first the Kingdom of God, secular matters will more or less look after themselves. It might also be called a doubly specialised statement of the general principle that all men (not only Europeans) should choose Christ (not only Christ-in-St. Benedict) as their leader or patron. I regard that choice as universally necessary; and there are of course other continents as well as Europe, other cultural traditions as well as that of the West, and other elements within Catholicism as well as the monastic element, all of them deserving high respect. But I am not concerned with these. My subject is the importance, for those particular people who are European or "Western" by inheritance, of that particular element in life and religion which we emphasise if we choose to call St. Benedict our "patron." I want to suggest that this importance is not simply a matter of past history on the one hand, or a matter of personal devotion and dedicated living on the other.

Any such suggestion will come up against one initial obstacle. It is often said that we live in a very materialistic and irreligious age. So we do, up to a point, and in so far as we do, the spirit of so deeply religious a man as St. Benedict is unlikely to seem very relevant to our future. But there is a danger of over-simplification here. What looks like a total abandonment of all religion may actually be, in certain cases, a relegation of religion to the strictly private and personal sphere, an exclusion of all religious considerations from those fields of public policy and public action in which our temporal future is decided. It seems probable to me that much of the so-called "materialism" of our time has this more complex nature in fact. The religious impulse, very broadly defined, is probably as universal as ever it was— full-blooded atheism is a rare thing. But we live in mostly pluralistic societies, within which "toleration" is treated as an absolute; and any society of that kind is bound to conduct its affairs on the basis of some broad economic and practical consensus, tolerating all religion so long as it remains the private concern of the individual whose tastes lie in that direction, but conceding it no public importance as a determinant of history. If it were conceded any importance of that kind, the principle of toleration would be at risk.

It would be a gross exaggeration to describe present-day Europe as totally materialistic, totally irreligious. None the less, it does conceive its corporate identity and the pattern of its future in secular terms, as is shown by the nature of its major institutions. In today's press, the very word "Europe" is regularly used as a kind of shorthand term, referring not to a geographical area nor to a religious and cultural tradition but, rather, to the European Economic Community—an organisation chiefly concerned with the maintenance and development of our present prosperity. (Many of my fellow countrymen, here in England, seem to think that "Europe" is mostly something to do with the price of butter.) Then there is NATO, a related but distinct organisation, Western if not strictly European; and I find it hard to believe that this is very much less materialistic. Ideally, perhaps, it ought to revive the spirit of the Crusades at their best, embodying the cause of Christ as against the godless totalitarianism that threatens from the East. The nature of modern armaments means that if it were so preoccupied in fact, it would face appalling problems of military morality. But I find it hard to believe that the motivation and drive behind NATO is so very religious in reality. It gets eagerly supported by men who care nothing for Christ, and even by some who are as totalitarian in principle as any Communist; overall, it seems to be chiefly a matter of prudential self-interest.

The pursuit of corporate self-interest—whether by economic or (under stringent conditions) by military means—cannot be regarded as an unmixed evil. But it is not what Christ was talking about, and it is not what St. Benedict was talking about; and so long as Europe sees its identity and its future in those terms, neither Christ nor St. Benedict will interest it very profoundly.

One's proper reply to this situation might be philosophical and theological: one might assert the reality and the greater importance of the things which Christ and St. Benedict *were* talking about, in the hope of re-converting Europe to the Faith that made it. That is indeed the overall purpose to which this book is intended to contribute obliquely. But as a first step, one can legitimately ask whether a pluralistic and secular Europe, neutral in all matters of religion, is likely to prove a sustainable thing—even at the practical and economic level which is its present concern.

It could fail to prove sustainable in two ways. In the first place, its religious or ideological neutrality might well prove illusory. The daily conduct of a society involves decisions, and these in turn involve value-judgments which, whether consciously or not, must necessarily presuppose one view or another of what human beings are and what human life is for. We may wish to prescind from all particular and debated questions of the religious kind, in a spirit of neutrality and consensus and toleration, but this is only a real option where trivial matters are concerned. On that kind of basis, we can certainly make good traffic-regulations and good public-health measures. But we cannot possibly devise a "value-free" policy for, say, education, or abortion, or euthanasia. In such matters as those, action (or, for that matter, inaction) necessarily depends upon belief. A society which shares a common faith will handle them according to value-judgments which are made consciously, on a public and agreed basis. But where a common faith is lacking, those value-judgments will still need to be made—the only difference is that they will now be made on some more or less unconscious, private, and controversial basis. Abolish some frank dogmatism and you do not find ideal neutrality taking over, you merely find some alternative and less candid dogmatism rushing in to fill the values-vacuum which you have created for it.

The three fields just mentioned—education, abortion, and euthanasia—illustrate this tendency very clearly. When society ceases to act on Christian principles, it adopts no real neutrality. It starts to act, instead, on the equally dogmatic principles of secular humanism.

There is a second and broader sense in which a pluralistic and secular Europe, neutral in religion, is likely to prove unworkable. Any such proposal depends essentially upon the assumption that religion *can* be made into a private matter, of no public and historical importance. But this is a very unrealistic assumption. History shows religion to be an explosive thing, a powerful and seldom predictable determinant of events; social anthropology shows it to be a social bond of the first importance, a necessary maker and sustainer of societies. What keeps any people in being is, above all, the fact that they have gods and temples in common, a shared religion or (if you prefer) a dominant myth which all accept. Lacking this, it will lack coherence and will soon collapse. The Communist world possesses the great practical advantage of having a dominant myth in common, one that works effectively as a social bond, even though it comes in several versions and is as cruel in practice as it is preposterous in theory. The great weakness of the West is that it has nothing comparable.

Pragmatically speaking, its future will depend upon its success in remedying this situation. The question of Europe's future is essentially the question of Europe's faith. If it continues to have no faith in common, it will have no future. The idea of a pluralistic and secular Europe, held together by nothing more than economic and military self-interest and achieving long-term stability on that kind of basis alone, is grossly implausible by any human and historical reckoning.

It might also be said to lack nobility, to enthrone ignoble values. Self-interest isn't enough for men.

*   *   *

In the later chapters of this book, I shall give various particular reasons for believing that a Europe which had St. Benedict as its effective patron, and lived accordingly, would be able to face its future with a good deal more confidence than most of us can sustain at present. In the meantime, I would like to offer three preliminary considerations, somewhat generalised, perhaps somewhat rhetorical, which point in the same direction and will help to bring the argument into clearer focus.

In the first place, it seems more than likely that we are now living through what future historians will call the final collapse of a great civilisation. If this looks like proving to be the case, and if "civilisation"—in any sense of that complex word—is something that we value, it follows that we ought to take an interest in anybody or anything of proved effectiveness in saving things from the wreck. And as I have already observed (it is a commonplace of history) the monastic institution of St. Benedict does have just that kind of proved effectiveness.

> Western monasticism entered into the heritage of the classical culture and saved it from the ruin that overwhelmed the secular civilisation of the Latin West at the end of the sixth century. It is to the monastic libraries and scriptoria that we owe the preservation and translation of almost the entire body of Latin classical literature that we possess today.

We look like needing that kind of talent again, and not only for the preservation of literary texts.

It might be needed, at one time or another, in any part of

the world. But St. Benedict is of particular value to ourselves, living in our particular part of the world. His Rule is followed fruitfully in every continent and by people of very different racial and cultural backgrounds. None the less, his outstanding effectiveness, as demonstrated by history, lies in the saving of European things from a European wreck. He is a major and most constructive part of our past; and if we now feel that we have somehow lost contact with our own roots and cannot decide which way to turn, if we feel uncertain how to save Europe, we might do well to turn back to that spirit and institution which, within the Church, did more than anything else to make Europe in the first instance.

We might define the problem by saying that Europe must re-discover its soul or else perish; and we might define the answer by saying that as a matter of history, the soul in question is essentially Catholic and very substantially Benedictine—my chief concern in this book being with this second aspect of it.

Finally, while all the saints are experts and exemplars in the art of good living, St. Benedict is something more specialised: he is probably history's greatest expert and exemplar in the art of good living *in community*. This is a notoriously difficult art—it often proves too much even for the best of men. St. Benedict's approach to it has been amply proved a realistic and effective one for mankind in general but especially for Europeans; and while he was primarily concerned with community living on a very small scale—with a family rather than a continent—his practical relevance (in this matter) is not confined to the cloister. "We cannot all be monks," said one writer on the Rule's value for laymen, "but it is to the monks that we must go, if we would learn once again the lost art of living in Christian community."

This is an art which we must indeed learn once more, if

the European community is to be anything more than a cynical and therefore doomed alliance of national egoisms; and if only for this reason, we would do well to make St. Benedict its effective patron.

*   *   *

At present, however, much of Europe seems to prefer other patrons. One of these is plainly Karl Marx; another is whatever prophet or deity presides over the cult of obsessive technological expansion and rabid consumerism, in its capitalist or semi-capitalist versions, and the associated cult of commercialised eroticism, graphic or musical. As I have observed, it would probably be an exaggeration to say that Europe or the West is post-Christian and irreligious in any thoroughgoing way. But so far as its public life and preoccupations are concerned, it seems to be poised between two materialisms which are equally violent, and equally alien to real human need, to our human and cultural tradition, and to Catholic Christianity.

This is an alarming situation, if only because neither of these two materialisms offers any future which is not ugly, violent, and despairing. I regard this as self-evidently true of any materialism of the Marxist kind. (If the reader thinks otherwise, this is the wrong book for him.) But it is only a shade less obvious that ugliness and violence and despair, patterned on slightly different lines, are characteristic also of those affluent Western societies which are still run on more or less capitalistic lines. For ugliness, you only need to look at their cities; for violence, you only need to read their newspapers or walk observantly in their streets; for despair, you only need to consider their arts, and also the probable future of the temporal prosperity—the ever-rising "standard of living"—to which most of their hope is currently directed.

(This isn't just a matter of the all-important oil giving out. It's that, and more crucially than most people are willing to see. But it's a great deal more as well: the good life, as currently conceived in the West, is unlikely to be available for very much longer. About the social and psychological consequences of its disappearance, it is hard to be optimistic.)

Stress and conflict appear to be the staples of our emerging future. None of Europe's present patrons offer it any real hope of the fourfold peace that we need: peace, first of all, with our non-human environment, with Nature; next, peace with our neighbours, with other men as we meet them; then, peace with our immeasurably difficult selves; and, finally and most decisively, peace with the ground of our being and of all being, peace with God.

Is any such fourfold peace attainable at all in this world? Certainly not under Europe's present patronage, and (one might suppose) not at all. What then? The fox in the fable, finding the grapes unattainable, decided that he didn't really want them. If you and I decide that peace is wholly beyond our reach, we are very likely indeed to settle for something else, for stress and conflict, while taking self-protecting care to be on the winning side if we can, the tough and unscrupulous side. If there is to be violence, we shall choose to be among those who inflict it, rather than among those who suffer it. Thus, almost innocently, as though in mere self-defence, we shall cast our practical vote for Hitler, for Stalin, for Mao, for Idi Amin, for all the bullies and murderers and tyrants whose incomplete but horribly excessive dominance has made history into the ugly mess which it always tends to be.

Can we, in practical terms, cast an effective vote any other way? Is there any alternative patron, any leader or *Führer* or *Duce*, who can really be trusted to lead Europe along the paths of that fourfold peace?

For that office, there is (in my view) only one plausible candidate: Jesus of Nazareth.

Absolutely speaking, there is no more to be said. But relatively speaking, historically speaking, psychologically speaking, there are certain points that still need to be added; and one of them concerns the particular road to Jesus that was mapped by St. Benedict and followed by his monks, ancient and modern. In the Father's house there are many mansions, and all roads lead to Rome: St. Benedict's particular mansion and road is the home and way for Europe, if indeed it really seeks that "peace" which the monks have chosen as their motto.

This may seem an arbitrary assertion. My purpose is to develop it in connection with a variety of Europe's present-day problems; and initially, in connection with our urgent need of "peace" at the primary level, as between ourselves and the natural or non-human world around us.

How badly, how violently we now treat that world, just as though it were an enemy! Did you catch an air of something more gentle and generous in that abbey where we began?

CHAPTER TWO

*A*t one time or another, most of us will have heard that celebrated piece of music called "In a Monastery Garden." It has a certain charm, though it is hardly to be reckoned among the masterpieces; the suggestion that it carries is of a faintly melancholic sweetness.

In carrying that suggestion, it reflects one widespread and not wholly erroneous notion of what monasticism is like. In the previous chapter, I mentioned three popular "images" of the monk. He can be seen as a pathetic character, mean-souled and miserable and perhaps masochistic; or as a grim fearsome character, austere and authoritarian, more than likely to burn you at the stake; or as a comic character, cheerfully self-indulgent like the rest of us while humor-ously pretending to be otherwise. But there is a fourth popu-lar "image" of him and his life. He is sometimes seen in sweet, sentimental, and nostalgic terms, as though he were primarily a man who lives dreamily in picturesque cloisters, thinking beautiful thoughts without effort, leaning pen-sively against ancient stone walls while the *Angelus* rings softly through the mellow light of an autumnal sunset—a man who has found rest and beauty where most of us have to live with stress and ugliness.

Does he really live in a kind of cloistered Garden of Eden? The idea that he does—by comparison with the rest of us, at any rate—has its appeal and therefore its popularity. If you asked a composer to write two separate pieces of music, one suggesting the monastic life and the other suggesting twentieth-century man's daily world of offices and factories and exhaust fumes and tranquillisers, you would end up with two sharply different compositions. One would speak of peace and beauty, the other of conflict and ugliness. Each would be valid in its way, and Ketelbey's message is not entirely deceptive.

It could deceive. A primarily aesthetic response to one's first experience of monasticism is understandable and entirely legitimate, but by no means sufficient. If any man decided to enter a monastery on that kind of basis, seeking there a life of pensive Epicurean simplicity in beautiful surroundings and an escape from stress and ugliness, he would sustain a rude shock when the novice master got to work on him. He wouldn't stay long. And if some casual lay visitor found himself overwhelmed by the sweet decorum of the monastic environment and took this to be the value for which it existed, he would be making a serious mistake.

But he would not be making a *total* mistake; he would be putting his finger on something important in its way, something which can serve as a starting-point for weightier considerations. I am concerned in this book with peace, and in this chapter with peace as between man and his environment or Nature; and this is a kind of peace which, when arduously pursued, does in fact establish beauty and has always done so. I do not regard aesthetic matters as having any primary kind of importance. But they deserve consideration, if only as pointing beyond themselves; and if our subject is the relevance of Benedictine life and values for present-day Europe, we may usefully begin with the aesthetic contrast between the cloister and the world. One's first experience of the cloister can be something of a shock. But it is usual, not exceptional, for the visitor to recover from that shock and then, if he has any sensitivity at all, to feel that he has there returned briefly to peace and civilisation and sanity from the barbarian desert within which he habitually lives without really noticing its violent and lunatic nature. Long familiarity has concealed this from his sight: the abbey opens his eyes, perhaps painfully at first, and then so reorientates his vision—in the direction of greater objectivity—that his own world, when he returns to it, horrifies him. "If my first days in the abbey had been a period of depression," says a writer already quoted, "the unwinding process, after I had left, was ten times worse. The abbey was at first a graveyard; the outer world seemed afterwards, by contrast, an inferno of noise and vulgarity entirely populated by bounders and sluts and crooks."

Is that perhaps a false and exaggerated response to the experience of leaving the cloister? The writer in question admits that it probably is; and there is obvious danger in any experience which disposes you to see *all* your fellow citizens as the bounders and sluts and crooks which some of them undoubtedly are. But that "inferno of noise and vulgarity" is hardly to be denied, especially if you live in some big violent city of the modern sort, and it suggests that we have lost the art, still retained and practised by the monks, of living gently and at peace with one's natural surroundings.

Can they help us to find it again?

* * *

Not long ago, I found myself walking around the ancient university city of Cambridge after an absence of some thirty years, and I was appalled by what I found. Here was a city devoted to learning and, until very recent times, to religion in equal or greater measure, as constituting the necessary base and framework for learning and indeed for all life; and for something like seven centuries, men had served these two noble purposes by erecting buildings, collegiate and ecclesiastical, of great variety but of consistent beauty. (Cambridge thus became a lovely place—lovelier even than

Oxford, perhaps, if an Oxford man can be allowed to make such a disloyal suggestion.)

During these last thirty years, the building process had continued, though mostly in the service of learning, now, and hardly at all of religion. And while these new structures were as varied as the old, I found them consistently hideous or, at the very best, drab and sterile and devoid of all beauty, all humanity, all interest. It was as though the hand of death had suddenly been laid upon a living and loved thing.

I should have been prepared for this shock, of course. The tendency in question is universal, and I had no reason to suppose that Cambridge would have escaped its influence. Go to almost any of the ancient cities of Europe, and you will find the same pattern. At the centre, you will find a few old buildings of great beauty, dating from the Middle Ages or perhaps earlier, with tourists gazing upon them very much as starving men gaze upon good food. Around these, you will find a ring of more recent buildings, less beautiful but still comely; and further out, there will be a spreading ocean of modern suburbs, more or less comfortable to live in as the case may be, but extremely poor in any kind of visual interest. But throughout—except (if the city fathers have been wise) in the mediaeval or older heart of the place—you will see the influence of two forces which have not merely failed to create beauty but seem to have aimed in some positive way at the creation of ugliness: industrialism on the one hand, and on the other, architecture of the aggressively "modern" kind, such as now abounds in Cambridge and in any other city you like to name.

If we are to consider the senses in which present-day Western man is at war with his environment, this is surely the most obvious though not necessarily the most important. The hand that he lays upon it is, visually, the hand of death. A remote English village is sometimes said to be "unspoilt": those who apply this word to it mean thereby that few of its buildings and other visible features are of this present age. By this familiar usage, they unconsciously concede a sadly embarrassing fact about ourselves. What is it that twentieth-century man most characteristically does to the countryside and its villages? He spoils them.

This is a new phenomenon. The fact that it is possible to make ugly artefacts, ugly buildings included, appears to have been a discovery of the early nineteenth century. Not only the great colleges and cathedrals of every earlier age but also the petty objects of its daily life—its pots and pans, its farm implements—possess a natural comeliness at the very least, such as is quite beyond our present reach, even when they are not "beautiful" in the more rarefied senses of that word. And things are naturally at their worst where the facts of history cause the more ancient centre to be simply absent. A New England village or small town—one in which the Colonial or Georgian manner of building is no forced and self-conscious revival but a continuing tradition—can be a pleasant place indeed. But the average American townscape is a kind of nightmare—though we Europeans are in an increasingly weak position to make superior comments upon this fact.

Economically speaking, present-day Western people live (by this world's standards, historical and geographical) like millionaires. But man does not live by bread alone; and in visually aesthetic terms, present-day Western people live like paupers. They are surrounded by gratuitous ugliness, made by themselves.

Various writers have considered this new situation, and it is widely agreed that the change which established it took place—not completely, but still crucially—during the first half of the nineteenth century. If we set out to consider the nature and causes of that change, two factors at least will seem of obvious relevance. One of them concerns the nature of work and of people's attitudes towards it. When the nineteenth century began, buildings and other artefacts were, predominantly, the direct work of human hands. They are now, predominantly, the output of mechanised industry, the service of which constitutes our primary understanding of what "work" means for most people; and by 1850, although this transition was by no means fully accomplished, it was sufficiently well advanced to constitute a visibly radical break with the whole of mankind's previous experience. Already by then, we had ceased to think of "work" as something which needs to be done for the common good and because idleness is the enemy of the soul, and as something from which a degree of satisfaction is normally to be expected. We were well on our way towards our modern understanding of such matters—our primarily negative concept of "work" as meaning an absence of unemployment, our assumption that "a job" is something which the individual is entitled to receive *from* the community rather than something which he does *for* the community, and our gloomy recognition that it will usually be monotonous and soul-destroying, filling the worker's time and providing him with a livelihood, but otherwise giving him little personal satisfaction or none. "Work," as so conceived, is an ugly thing, and we need not be surprised if ugliness is among its characteristic products.

Throughout the West, that same period—roughly from 1800 to 1850—was also marked by a sharp decline in the influence of religious considerations and religious institutions. In the England of Dr. Johnson's day, while people naturally differed in belief and devotion and morality, it remains true that most of them instinctively saw the human situation and the business of life in primarily religious terms, as Western man had done for millennia and as "primitive" people still do. But by the time Matthew Arnold came to write *Dover Beach*, the situation had altered radically: the agnostic and secular world had started to emerge, and the "ages of faith" now seemed like a dream of distant childhood as remembered in the tiredness of middle age.

Inevitably, this great change had its cultural and aesthetic repercussions, and they still continue. François Mauriac once observed that the problems of the novel, in his day, stemmed from the modern concept of man—a concept which, he said, was totally negative. This was one instance of a wider truth. Whatever notion men have of themselves and their destiny is going to find expression in the novel and also in the other arts, and notably in architecture, which is the most visually inescapable of them all. When Christianity was the common faith, it was also a stupendously fruitful influence upon artistic creativity in every mode; and if the West had turned from it to some alternative but still positive faith, the cultural loss might well have been limited. Islamic influence, for example, could have borne rich fruit among us in due time. But in fact, and most decisively in that early part of the nineteenth century, the West turned from Christianity to something overwhelmingly negative, to the religious and philosophical nihilism that now prevails, to a scepticism that allows only one single dogma—the idea that human beings are nothing so special, that *Homo sapiens* is a highly developed mammalian species and no more.

From our adoption of this sceptical nihilism and this very low view of ourselves, it followed quite naturally that our arts would become sterile and despairing and our physical environment hideous. If Cambridge (as I used to know it) was lovely, this is because it was built by men who believed in Christ. The trouble about those new buildings, erected there during these last thirty years, is that they were built by men who believed in nothing at all.

*   *   *

The first responses of the visitor to some present-day

monastery may indeed be aesthetic: what strikes him, once the initial shock is over, may well be the beauty of the place and of the life led there by the monks. But his enquiring mind will then lead him to consider the roots or sources of this, and he will make two preliminary observations about how monks differ from other men. The first is that they very definitely do *not* believe in "nothing at all." They are men of total commitment to a specific and fully-worked-out Faith which has stood the test of time, and while they are unlikely to be argumentative men, there are those among them who are fully capable of defending and justifying that Faith against any opposition of the most formidably intellectual kind. The second is that they attach a positive value to work. For them, it is neither a personal entitlement nor yet a meaningless burden: they see it as a practical necessity for the common good, yes, but also as a prime means for the maintenance of the individual's psychological and spiritual health. And this perspective governs the nature and motivation of the work they do. They have no desire to lay the aggressive hand of death upon their environment. They are at peace with it, and it is from this first grade or order of peace that the beauty stems which first struck the visitor.

It is a fact of common experience. A tragic episode in history means that, for many English people, the word "abbey" is first and foremost suggestive of a *ruined* abbey, Fountains or Tintern or Rievaulx, envisaged always as a place of haunting beauty, all the more intense by reason of its tragic dimension. But monastic architecture in all its variety—ranging from the austere dignity associated with the Cistercian tradition to the jubilant richness of the baroque—does not in any way depend upon that elegiac suggestion of vanished glories: its impact will be greatest where the abbey is most alive, its community most numerous, their dedication and worship and observance most punctilious. There, rather than among the ruins, it will strike the visitor with the greatest force, making him realise—possibly for the first time—that even in this twentieth century, day-to-day life does not *have* to be lived meaninglessly and in hideous surroundings.

That realisation can of course strike him elsewhere: something like it may be in the minds of those tourists who come to gaze upon the mediaeval buildings, sacred or secular, of Cambridge or any other ancient European city. But even there, the influence of St. Benedict will be at work. Those mediaeval buildings are only a tourist-attraction because they are in fact worth looking at, in simple admiration and perhaps in nostalgia and a kind of envy; and they have this character because they grew out of the culture of the high Middle Ages—a culture which, although primarily rooted in the Catholic Faith as such, received its historical formation during those "Benedictine centuries" when the monastery was the dominant social institution and the primary determinant of cultural life. Among the complex factors which make up the hauntingly sweet atmosphere of, say, Bruges or Salzburg, one of the most perceptible is a background fragrance of the *pax Benedictina*.

Something similar has been claimed for the Church of England, curiously but (in my view) plausibly. Without wishing to offend any Anglican readers, I am unconvinced by their claim to be fully and organically within the Universal Church. But if any man grew up in the English countryside, was soaked from an early age in English literature, and completed his education at Oxford, he would need to lack all sensitivity if he were not to feel a powerful *attrait* to the Anglican *ethos*. I have just that background and I feel just such an *attrait*, rather as a virtuous married man might feel drawn to some woman who is not for him. And I tend to agree with those writers who see the *ethos* in question, partly at least, as a lingering presence of that Benedictine spirit which had such a very formative influence upon the English Catholicism of the Middle Ages.

I detect a kind of continuity there—one which, unlike some others of greater importance, survived the Reformation. I do not believe that the Anglican clergyman is what I call a "priest," except in certain rather exceptional cases. But there are cultural and psychological senses, important at their own level, in which he and his whole background tradition remind me sharply of the monks. He has my high regard in consequence, and even my love.

*   *   *

God made a beautiful world, and the monks—being at peace with it—characteristically enhance its beauty, where "the modern world" shows a consistent tendency to make it hideous. Within our overall concern for Europe's future, there will surely be (in its proper place) an aesthetic element: we shall want this varied and lovely continent to be, in every obvious sense, a pleasant place to live in. But if we do, we shall have to undertake some very radical rethinking. All present tendencies operate in the converse sense: day by day, Europe is taking upon itself more and more of that urban and technological ugliness which mars the American scene, and without acquiring the American virtues by way of counter-balance.

This, in itself, might be a sufficient reason for giving renewed and sympathetic attention to a Rule and a way of life which have contributed so substantially to most of what we value in Europe. But we have a further reason for doing so, a practical and most urgent reason, and one less open to charges of mere aestheticism and sentimentality. Where men fail to live at peace with their natural environment, they are indeed likely to generate ugliness. But they will also find themselves at war with the physical and biological basis of their own existence: they will be endangering their own survival.

If Europe needs St. Benedict for its patron, this is partly because, like the West in general, it now faces a high probability of disaster—ecological and economic in the first instance, but with social and political consequences of the ugliest kind; and it seems that the dangers in question will only be averted by a rediscovery and an assiduous practice of certain unfashionable virtues, natural and Christian but also, in a very specific way, monastic.

The point is that personal expectations have risen to a level at which they can almost certainly not be sustained for much longer. Some people still talk as though the "affluent society" and the life style enjoyed by so many in the prosperous West during the last twenty-five years represented some kind of permanent destiny, to which all men could aspire. But this now seems more likely to prove a local, freakish, and temporary thing, made briefly possible by the phenomenally rapid destruction of non-renewable resources, and of fossil fuels in particular.

It is as well to remember that we are still only human beings, still subject to the raw human condition: we still belong to the same species as the Bushmen of the Kalahari, or the aborigines of the Gibson Desert in Australia, or the neolithic men who once roamed the Berkshire hills of my childhood, and God has signed no kind of contract that we are always going to live much more comfortably than them. We may possibly contrive to do so, in some degree at least. If we don't, things will be (by our present standards) extremely tough, and this will be regrettable. But we will not have suffered an injustice. We have no divine entitlement to a "high standard of living," in the sense of an extremely rapid consumption of industrial goods and services and therefore of natural resources.

But the idea that we do have such an entitlement seems to be widespread, and in this fact, there are bad omens for the future. Most people can stand up to simple hardship and respond to it with fortitude. But when hardship is conceived as injustice, when people feel that they have been cheated of their natural rights, a different response is usual: bitterness, and the sins of envy and anger, and violence all too often.

For a wide variety of ecological and economic reasons—concerned initially with the availability and price of oil—it seems that Europe's present "standard of living" is unlikely to be sustainable for very much longer: for affluent Western man in general, the party is pretty well over. In the purely physical sense, this won't be too disastrous: we don't really *need* our present multiplicity of goods and services—colossal efforts in advertising and salesmanship are necessary to make us buy them—and they do not make us particularly happy.

But can the party end peacefully? It is hard to see how it can, so long as its questionable pleasures are regarded as a natural entitlement, owing in justice to every man. Where that mentality prevails, any decline in the "standard of living" will be met not with fortitude but with bitterness: it will be seen as a cheat and injustice—or at best as a culpable failure—on the part of some evil "Them." Envy and anger will prevail; extensive violence is all too probable.

In view of these dangers, Europe would be well advised to learn from the monks, and in at least two respects.

In the first place, if we say that the monk lives at peace with the natural world around him, we mean that he lives rather simply, rather abstemiously. To use the ecological jargon of our time: he makes limited demands upon his natural environment and imposes a limited load upon it. His reasons for doing so are initially spiritual and ascetic, but our reasons for imitating him are practical or prudential as well.

It is important here to invoke the patronage of St. Benedict, rather than of holy men in general, since it is part of his distinctive wisdom to speak in the language of moderation. All things are possible to God, but not all things are probable among men: one can aspire to a certain change in Europe's heart and therefore its direction, but no recommendation for its future is going to be very practical if it demands sustained heroism from the mass of ordinary people. If we all started to live like Trappists, most of our economic problems would disappear overnight. But the Trappist life is an extremely austere one and the Trappist vocation is correspondingly rare—you and I and our neighbours are unlikely to rise to any comparable heights. But St. Benedict's way, if not exactly easy, is not for heroes alone.

This point deserves attention, within the cloister and elsewhere. Throughout the world, religious man has always recognised the need for a certain asceticism: self-indulgence does not need to be very gross before it becomes, unmistakably, an enemy of the soul. But there is a converse danger. Asceticism can itself become a passion, and even a subtly disguised and perverse form of self-indulgence—it can express a Manichaean hatred of the body or a pathological tendency towards masochism. And even where these dangers are avoided, it can cause religion to have so very austere and forbidding an"image" as to deter the ordinary man and perhaps fill him with despair. It may speak too insistently of the Cross, and insufficiently of the sweet yoke and the light burden.

Part of St. Benedict's importance, for the history of monasticism, lies in his recognition of the fact that the urge to asceticism, like our other natural urges, is good in itself but needs to be tempered and disciplined. Here, as elsewhere, excess and extravagance can be discouraging and otherwise harmful, as was obvious from the record of certain earlier monks and hermits. St. Benedict therefore wrote a *gentle* Rule—one in which, he hoped, nothing would prove too difficult for the ordinary man who was no hero but sought an education in the Lord's service. In a healthy abbey of the present day, therefore, his monks do not "live well" as an affluent society might understand that expression. But they do not live so very badly, either. Theirs is a tempered asceticism. It is alien to the fanatical Puritanism of those who swear that nobody must ever eat meat or drink wine.

But it is equally alien to the pig-like gluttony of those who demand twelve-inch steaks and buckets of hard liquor upon every occasion, as though by right. It carries a clear message about the whole of life, not only about food and drink. A good man may legitimately make certain demands upon the physical and biological world around him: it is not a mortal sin to eat beef or use electricity or travel by jet, or to look forward to doing such things in the future. But all such demands and expectations need to be very limited, very tempered, very conditional, cherished only in the most light and humorous way. If we are deeply upset and made angry by any frustration or disappointment in these matters, there will be something seriously wrong with us—we shall be in a predatory and therefore false relationship with God's creation.

The monk is not miserable or half-starved. But his dominant values are very unlike those of a society whose basic attitude to the world around it is greedily predatory rather than peaceful; and if Europe could only be persuaded to follow his example—in the gentle spirit of St. Benedict, and not necessarily to any heroic degree—the prospects for its temporal as well as its spiritual future would be very much improved.

There is a second and more particular respect in which the

Benedictine monk (as distinct from wise and holy men in general) sets an example which we would do well to follow. There is a certain disease from which Europe (and not *only* Europe) is now suffering most grievously; and if the monk is not wholly immune to it, he is at least making a determined effort to recover from it. He recognises its pathological nature. It can be summed up as a neurotic addiction to mobility, to transportation, to the fret and turmoil of always being on the move from here to there. Almost uniquely in this age, the monk is happy to stay at home.

He thereby displays a specifically Benedictine wisdom. It is not the only possible wisdom. In every kind of monastic or religious tradition, including those which are not Catholic or Christian at all, there has always been an element of asceticism and poverty, more or less extreme as the case may be; and the poverty in question has sometimes been that of the man who lacks a home and must always be wandering. Ideally at least, the Jesuit or Franciscan is a man who puts down no roots: his bag is always packed and is a light one anyway, he is always ready to move off to the other end of the town or the other end of the world.

In practice, something similar can be true of the Benedictine monk, occasionally at least. You must not be very surprised if you meet him at the airport, but you should be *slightly* surprised. He is there exceptionally, not characteristically. Alone among religious people, he has taken a vow of "stability."

This word has several meanings. It implies, for one thing, that the monk has committed himself to perseverance: he is not going to abandon his vocation when it becomes tedious, as it probably will, sooner or later, for a time at least. It also implies that he has committed himself to the life and work and obedience of one specific house, rather than of some flexible and world-wide organisation—even though the house in question may keep sending him off to the railway station or the airport. He obeys when so commanded. But for him, in principle, there is something unfortunate and undesirable about railway stations and airports, and even about any wild, reckless walking. He follows St. Benedict, who had some severe things to say about the *gyrovagus*, the monk with itchy feet. When he took that vow of stability, he was expressing, among other things, his conviction that it's a good thing to stay at home.

This is indeed only a partial wisdom and one among many. But it is a wisdom that Europe needs in this age of obsessive mobility, since it is a mode of peace with one's surroundings. "The truest and most horrible claim made for modern transport," said C. S. Lewis, "is that it 'annihilates space'. It does. It annihilates one of the most glorious gifts we have been given." Your car—Lewis was rejoicing in the fact that his father never had one—is a mode of destructiveness, of aggression.

*   *   *

The monk lives stably and at peace with God's world; most of us live restlessly and are at war with it, thus putting ourselves more seriously at risk than we want to admit.

The ecological or environmental problem facing the West is only taken lightly by those who have not paid serious attention to the facts, or who place unwarranted faith in the ability of human cleverness to resolve absolutely any problem which confronts it. It can resolve a great many problems; it may, conceivably, be able to resolve the problem of environmental pollution. But it cannot possibly confer permanence upon any way of life which depends crucially upon the increasingly rapid consumption of non-renewable resources.

During the last ten or fifteen years, a great deal has been

written about the relationship between our explosively-developing technology and the world upon which we all depend, and a certain degree of agreement seems to have been reached, though with various qualifications in one quarter or another. To grasp the broad picture, one need only consider the expression "Man's Conquest of Nature." It is in some such terms as those that present-day Western society most naturally conceives the principal business of life. For most older wisdoms, Christian and pagan, Nature or the earth was primarily our mother, our friend, our fellow-creature under God. But for us, it has become an enemy, something to be conquered and beaten down and pillaged without scruple in our own selfish interest: we want to suck its blood, we want to consume its limited wealth more and more rapidly, with no regard for its own autonomous dignity or even for the needs of our own descendants.

And so, at a headlong pace, we cause life to become ever more complex, technological, urban, destructive, and wasteful. Our nominal reason for doing this is a desire that hyper-consumerism and affluence should develop without limit and come to prevail everywhere. We like to think that this whole programme is charitable in nature, ordered towards the well-being and happiness of all mankind. But on closer examination, any such interpretation of our current behaviour turns out to lack plausibility. As Jacques Ellul has argued very convincingly, technological development seems to proceed causally, not teleologically: it is neither friendly nor hostile to human well-being, but simply irrelevant to it. The supersonic passenger aircraft provides us with a supreme instance of this. It is a miracle of human ingenuity, and it is almost totally pointless. It enables small numbers of rich men to save very small amounts of time when travelling. But nobody could argue seriously—and few people have tried to argue in fact—that in terms of general human well-being, this tiny benefit justifies so colossal an investment of resources and dedication. The thing was built because it had become possible to build it.

Beyond this, it is becoming increasingly obvious that while great poverty is a bitter and painful thing, the converse is far from being true. Hyper-consumerism and affluence do not lead to happiness. Where these things prevail most lavishly—in the United States, for example, or in Sweden—they tend to be accompanied by correspondingly high levels of psychological and social stress, as measured by the sad statistics of suicide and mental breakdown.

But we still press on blindly, burdening ourselves with an endless succession of new and largely fictitious needs, simply in order to justify our continual escalation of this furiously exploitative war against Nature and against stability in particular. When families have to be evicted and farms obliterated for the sake of some new motorway or some new airport, how many of us question the purposes and priorities thereby implied?

* * *

All this calls for comment which may well be psychological in the first instance, a matter of motivation. *Why* does modern Western man commit himself so passionately to a pattern of behaviour and a style of life which fails so conspicuously to make him happy and which, by its very impermanence, threatens him with major disaster in the near future? Why is it only small minorities who seek a more peaceful and sustainable and even a more monastic life style? Mere greedy self-indulgence is obviously involved in some degree. But there is more to it than that.

In an earlier book (*The Delicate Creation*), I put forward the idea that modern man's technological "Conquest of

Nature"—his treatment of God's world as though it were an enemy—has one quasi-religious motivation among others. It can be seen as a new and not explicitly theological version of certain very ancient heresies, Gnostic and Manichaean, which have tended to recur in one form or another down the centuries. It makes great sense, on the face of it, to regard the visible universe as an imperfect or even a thoroughly bad thing—the work of blind forces if not of some demiurge or devil. The notorious problem of evil creates familiar difficulties for those who want to regard our world as the handiwork and property of a personal God who is infinite in both love and power. If we see it as an enemy rather than a friend and treat it accordingly, we have at least an apparent case for doing so. The Cross of Christ is God's answer to the problem of evil. But where the Cross is rejected or ignored, hostility towards Nature—and even an active war against it—follows quite naturally and even (in a sense) logically. If the old Manichees did not conduct that war as effectively as we can, this is only because they lacked the means. They certainly had the motivation.

If we are to live at peace with the world around us, the first necessity is that we should recognise its ontological goodness and even its holiness, which dimly reflects that of its Creator. This is a matter of theology and faith; the Rule of St. Benedict takes it for granted.

Then, if we consider our society's passionate concern for economic matters, its elevation of hyper-consumerism and affluence into absolute values and of luxuries into necessities, we may well be reminded of a certain familiar fact about adolescent behaviour. It is, unfortunately, no rare thing for a growing boy to be in a bad relationship with his father. Typically, he will then seek comfort in over-eating. He will become greedy. Cakes, buns, sweets, appalling chemical drinks—he will force them all down, hardly noticing their flavour, deriving no real pleasure from them and doing no good at all to his health, but with a kind of desperation driving him on.

If we know of any such sad case, we shall desire that boy to be reconciled to his father—mostly for the obvious human reasons, but also because as things now stand, food is being wasted and health imperilled. Can we not respond in a similar way to the "consumer society" of today? In its practice of obsessive grab and gobble, should we not see, first of all, evidence of its bad relationship with its Father? And is not the unappreciative waste of good resources, important in its way, a real matter for sadness among the other and more important aspects of that bad relationship?

A Benedictine monk is, above all, a man who seeks to be in a good relationship with his Father. In so far as he succeeds, his tempered abstemiousness becomes a matter of no great effort. He loses the urge to grab and gobble; he doesn't *need* to be so graspingly aggressive towards the natural world around him. But it also works the other way round. If he tries to make peace with that natural world and refrain from gobbling and grabbing at it, this is initially his way of breaking the chains of self-indulgence and self-love which have hitherto kept him aloof and estranged from the Father.

And it is in that same spirit that he will take his vow of "stability"—in all the senses of that word, but most notably (for our present purposes) in the sense of repudiating the values and behaviour of "the highway society," the neurotic twitch and scurry of endless and largely pointless movement which characterises our present world and uses up such a phenomenal quantity of our limited and precious oil. He will not see this, precisely, as a sin. But he will see it as a great foolishness and distraction, a huge collective attempt to escape from the oppressive burdens of reality and self, and one which was foredoomed to failure from the start, as pagan wisdom told us long ago.

Caelum non animum mutant qui trans mare currunt,
Strenua nos exercet inertia: navibus atque
Quadrigis petimus bene vivere. Quod petis hic est,
Est Ulubris, animus si te non deficit aequus.

"That big intercontinental flight will bring you to a different sky but not a different self. You and all of us work frenziedly at nothing at all: we behave as though 'the good life' was a matter of power-boats and fast cars, of getting somewhere else at high speed. A great mistake! What you're looking for is *here*, right here at Puddleby or Podunk, if only you wouldn't throw away your peace of mind."

*　　*　　*

There is indeed much to be said for the monk's way, which involves staying at home and striking roots and seeking the ultimate and unimaginable Good in peace of mind and within oneself. The case for such a life style is primarily spiritual: "Those who go much abroad seldom grow in sanctity," says the *Imitation of Christ*, and the "going abroad" in question need not involve any crossing of frontiers, any showing of passports. But St. Benedict's expression of the same principle associates it with a very distinctive attitude towards the practical economics of life— an attitude sharply different from that which mostly prevails in present-day Europe. The monastery, he says, "ought if possible to be so constituted that all things necessary, such as water, a mill, and a garden, and the various crafts may be contained within it; so that there may be no need for the monks to go abroad, for this is by no means expedient for their souls."

The monk (in other words) should not only live rather abstemiously, but also on a basis which approximates as closely as possible to local self-sufficiency. In historical fact, his practice has varied. You can sometimes find monasteries in large cities, and you can often find monks whose particular work causes them to be, in whatever degree, dependent like the rest of us upon the appallingly fragile complexities of long-distance trade and international finance, and upon the adversary-relationship with Nature entailed by these things. But all such cases are anomalous. Ideally and often in simple fact, the monk is at peace with God's world because the economics of his life are simple and, therefore, stable and sustainable: he observes a kind of practical wisdom which most of us have rejected in favour of aggressiveness and greed and ever-increasing complexity, thereby putting ourselves seriously and needlessly at risk.

The practical wisdom in question is not of course peculiar to the monks. Until modern methods of transport became available, most people had to live mostly on local resources, if only for lack of any alternative. But any great reluctance to do so is "irreligious" in the widest possible sense, as well as being irrational and imprudent. The wise men of all faiths have recognised this, and a very influential Catholic writer of our own time chose to state the matter in terms of what he called "Buddhist economics." From that point of view, said E. F. Schumacher,

> production from local resources for local needs is the most rational way of economic life, while dependence upon imports from afar and the consequent need to produce for export to unknown and distant peoples is highly uneconomic and justifiable only in exceptional cases and on a small scale.... The Buddhist economist would hold that to satisfy human wants from faraway sources rather than from sources nearby signifies failure rather than success.

It also signifies conflict, with Nature in the first instance and, in all probability, with other men before long; and for the purposes of Europe and the West in general, we can adapt that profoundly wise observation by reading "monastic" or "Benedictine" where Schumacher wrote "Buddhist." The wisdom there indicated is indeed "religious," but in a natural rather than a specifically Christian sense. Within our tradition, St. Benedict is its great preacher and his monks are its great practitioners.

* * *

My subject is the future of Europe, and the pattern which this might take if we made St. Benedict into our effective patron. At present, our governing values are about as un-monastic as they could possibly be; and it would be Utopian and unrealistic to look for any sudden and universal change of heart, especially if this involved any sustained practice of extreme asceticism by the bulk of ordinary people. As I have observed, the Trappist vocation is a rare one.

But the Benedictine vocation is a good deal less rare, and some modest lay or secular version of it can be advanced, without any fanciful romanticism, as an entirely practical school in which a significant number of us might learn the great fourfold lesson of peace—and initially, of peace with the world around us—so effectively as to be influential and even decisive for the European future.

What would happen then?

There would be no grand revolution, but there would be a number of slow, subtle shifts in emphasis. So far as the theme of this chapter is concerned, the first of these would be an increased willingness to live rather more simply. At the very least, we would stop regarding the multiplication of needs and the consequent furious exploitation of Nature as automatically good. We would no longer waste resources quite as recklessly as we now do, and fewer of us would die of over-eating. Then, we would pay greater attention to every man's need of a real usefulness rather than of a mere "job." While wishing to minimise mere drudgery, we would see work in positive terms, distrusting all such technologies as tend to make men useless. Our instinct would be for economic and other decentralisation, for local or regional self-sufficiency in essentials at least, and we would attach less importance than we now do to large-scale transportation, of commodities and of people as well: we would become increasingly bored by motorways and airports, increasingly appreciative of home and neighbourhood. By present-day standards, our lives and our loyalties would become more agrarian and rural, less industrial and urban. We would treat the fertile land—the earth, our mother—with enormous care and reverence. Fewer and fewer of us would consent to the sterile tedium of office or factory work. More and more of us would demand the satisfaction of actually making useful things with our hands, and one consequence of this would be that we would start to produce beautiful artefacts once again, beautiful buildings in particular. Among constructional materials, we would lose our present attachment to concrete; among colours, we would lose our present attachment to dismal grey. To our cities and villages, we could then do things that would be a matter for pride, and not (like the things we now do to them) a matter for humiliation and shame.

A degree of optimism, on such lines as these, will become realistic in so far as we start to treat our European environment on lines somewhat more monastic, somewhat more Benedictine. It cannot be an unqualified optimism. In any such future, the average man's life would become slightly more arduous, physically speaking, than it is today. But this would make it healthier; and psychologically speaking, it would be a great deal more rewarding. We would have come fruitfully to terms with our surroundings: we would have rediscovered—imperfectly, no doubt, but substantially—that particular element in the cloister's serenity which stems from the fact that the monks do not despise and fight and exploit God's world, but are at peace with it.

CHAPTER THREE

$\mathcal{R}$obert Browning—a "romantic" in many senses of that word—wrote a poem which is both entertaining and horrifying as a statement of pure malevolence. In nine stanzas, short and characteristically elliptic in language, it represents the inner thoughts of a man who is obsessed by festering hatred towards a colleague, and who expresses this by constant petty acts of spite: he even dreams of pulling off some trick that will secure the eternal damnation of his detested enemy, whose absolute vileness—it's completely invisible to the reader—is the only thing he can think about. In himself, of course, he sees nothing but good.

One reads this poem, perhaps, with amusement. It seems like a grotesque exaggeration, a caricature. But it isn't really so funny. In hatred—and even hatred of this "pure" kind, unrelated to real injuries and grievances—we must reluctantly recognise a recurring element in human psychology and behaviour, one which operates at various levels and generates an enormous amount of unnecessary conflict and suffering. It can arise within the family, and hideously; it can arise as between individuals and groups and classes, within the local or national community; and it can arise as between nations or empires, and will then often lead to mutual slaughter on the grand scale, while each side protests its total innocence and its overwhelming desire for peace.

Our European past, in particular, has been characterised—to a degree which Christian people must regard as shameful—by hatred and violent conflict at each of these three levels, and most notably by two major wars in this century alone. The fact that we are not actually fighting one another at the present time, with guns and tanks and bombs, should not delude us into supposing that we have solved the problem of how to live at peace with one another, which is quite as serious as the problem of how to live with the natural and non-human world around us, if not more so. The passions which exploded in 1914 and 1939 are still active, though quiescent, and comparable stresses still exist within family and social life. At all levels, our future depends crucially upon our success in establishing peace as between man and man.

Here again, it is my contention that we have much to gain from an effective adoption of St. Benedict's patronage. In his Rule and the life of his monks (who have "Peace" for their motto) we can find a lesson and a model, somewhat unfashionable perhaps, but as relevant and practical outside the cloister as within.

Some might think otherwise. Monks are not necessarily perfect men, and one does not need to be an extreme cynic to recognise that religious people have a distinct tendency to quarrel among themselves, often furiously. Ecclesiastical history is very largely a record of contention, and monastic history includes an element of the same kind. The devils of hatred and discord are very hard to kill, and I myself have detected their presence within certain cloisters which I shall not name. Some people even regard the presence and power of those devils as characteristic of the cloister: monks (they feel) are bitter and frustrated people, cramped in an unnatural life style, subject to unnecessary tensions, inevitably disposed therefore to spite and malevolence among themselves. Something of this sort was in Browning's mind when he wrote the poem already mentioned. It is called "Soliloquy of the Spanish Cloister," and the savage hatred which fills

it is that of one monk towards another. Browning may
have been intending some kind of smug insular accusation
against Spain; he was certainly intending some kind of
smug Protestant accusation against monasticism.

It is important to avoid romantic illusion, and to recognise
the element of truth within that accusation. If the monks are
to be regarded as our experts and mentors in the arts of living
together at peace, this is not because they have chosen an
easy way and found total success. They have in fact chosen
an extremely difficult way: they have engaged with what
may be called "the social problem" at a depth and intensity
which few of us could tolerate, venturing far into a most
dangerous and painful country in order to garner the
practical wisdom which we can now learn from them on
relatively easy terms.

The point is that the "social problem" is essentially that of
conflicting egoisms. In the outside world, the impact of this
fact is blunted for most of us by all manner of distractions,
economic and political and so forth. Unless we are very holy
indeed, there will be something within us that responds at
once, almost eagerly, to Sartre's ugly observation that "Hell
is other people." We see these alien creatures as competitors
and enemies, and it is our instinct to fight them and assert
self against them. But circumstances usually enable us to
evade or soften any full confrontation with them. We can at
least choose our friends, and avoid such people as arouse our
hostility most sharply. To some degree, we can usually
choose the colleagues among whom we spend our working
lives. We certainly choose our wives or husbands; and in
general, family life is helped along very substantially by the
natural ties of sexual and parental affection. Even when
things turn difficult, change and movement and variety can
bring us some relief. If we define the "social problem" as the
problem of how to live together without tearing one
another's eyes out, most of us manage to face only an eased

and palliated version of it. We don't all perform so very splendidly, even so.

The monk faces that same problem in a pure or absolute version, and all the more exactingly because of the absence of distractions: the mechanical and practical and economic business of life is already settled for him, a matter of smooth-running routine, absorbing little or none of that fighting instinct which all men have until they kill it, leaving him simply, almost nakedly, face to face with his neighbour, whom he may or may not then fight. His vocation (in part) is that of loving him and not fighting him. Its tremendous difficulty needs to be recognised.

In order to indicate the nature of this difficulty, let us bring a cautious cynicism to bear upon a fact of common observation which is sometimes interpreted rather too sentimentally. Anyone who visits a monastery for the first time is likely to comment upon the manifest happiness of the monks. I take this to be an entirely genuine happiness, usually at least, though of a complex kind. But one needs to remember that in the nature of the case, the visitor only meets a monk at a time when the monk is meeting a visitor; and if his face is wreathed in smiles, it may be partly for that reason. A visitor! A new face! A different person! The possibility, at least, of hearing some utterance—even if it's only a small joke—which one hasn't heard a million times already!

In order to perceive the joy of such a moment—from the monk's point of view—imagine that you have been sentenced to live permanently, within a fairly restricted environment, in close contact with a more or less unchanging group of people. You did not choose their company as a man chooses his friends, and they are bound to you by no ties of kinship. They do change slowly and imperceptibly: new faces appear from time to time, old faces disappear into the grave. But for the most part it's just the same too-familiar people, the same old mannerisms and eccentricities, experienced yesterday and today and tomorrow in the context of a rigid unchanging routine. How can you possibly endure it? The trouble isn't that they're bad, or hostile to yourself, or anything like that. It lies in the mere fact of their separate individuality, when caused to impinge upon you so remorselessly. Other people—even *good* other people—can indeed become a kind of Hell. That curious quirk of Brother Lawrence's behaviour, for example—it seemed rather entertaining and endearing when you first met him, but after twenty-five years, it may come close to driving you insane. (And you may completely fail to notice that corresponding quirk or mannerism of your own which is having the same effect upon him.)

Most of us would find such a life completely intolerable. The monks do not play down its extreme difficulty. They live penitentially in various ways; but the authorities of their tribe agree that the greatest penance of all lies in the mere fact of common life in a monastery, and we can agree with them. Which of us would not gladly embrace the utmost in physical austerities if the alternative was an obligation to hear—once again, and for the millionth time in twenty-five years—that infuriatingly characteristic cough and giggle of Brother Lawrence as he shuffles into the refectory?

The remarkable thing is that despite a way of life which might be expected to make men turn mad and murderous in mutual irritation, monasteries are usually very serene and peaceful places. The monk may indeed be glad to meet a visitor and so enjoy a brief holiday from the social monotony of his life, but this will still be rather like the brief holiday that a fish might take from the water in which he is at home, and he will be even more glad to return to that cloistered monotony and the unchanging company of his brethren. Against all the odds, he is at peace with them. The social problem, faced by these men in an exceptionally acute version, has been solved by them with exceptional success.

* * *

In our own interest, we in the outside world would do well to consider the nature and basis of that success. We need its secret. Whatever factors generate peace in the cloister may be capable of adaptation, so as to generate the same blessing elsewhere—within the family, the country, the international European scene.

How *do* monks manage to live together at peace?

Two initial answers to that question can be dismissed briefly—not as being unimportant, but as having only limited relevance to our present theme.

In the first place, while the problem of peace arises in an exceptionally acute version within the cloister, it arises there as between men who are themselves rather unusual. I have already observed that they are very ordinary men. But they are ordinary men who have taken a distinctly unusual decision: they have all resolved to dedicate their entire lives to the vowed pursuit of goodness, of Christ, of God, and therefore to the systematic fighting-down of that assertive egoism with which all of us are born and which generates so large a proportion of this world's stress and violence. They therefore constitute an un-typical sample of the human race, and one which is heavily biassed—if I may put it like that— in the direction of peace. Except when they venture forth, they only need to live immediately at peace with other monks. In sharp contrast, you and I must somehow manage to live at peace with a wide variety of people, many of them committed very weakly indeed—if at all—to the service of Christ and the cause of peace, some of them very conspicuously committed to competitive self-assertion and aggressiveness. Our task, in some ways easier than that of the monks, is therefore more difficult in other ways. This fact does not mean that monastic virtues and values are irrelevant to life outside the cloister. But we must allow it to modify our expectations. Europe is not going to become a kind of super-monastery, entirely populated by individuals who have chosen to live by monastic standards of self-renunciation and goodness. Its varied and colourfully imperfect peoples are therefore unlikely to achieve the supreme peace which characterises the cloister. That's for the specialists. Never-theless, even a small step in its direction would make our lives a great deal better and happier and our newspapers a great deal more dull.

If the monks' peacefulness stems partly from the fact that each of them only has other monks to live with, it also stems, crucially, from that powerful but mysterious force which Christians call "the grace of God." Without this, all human attempts to live the good life in common show a consistent tendency to fail, often disastrously. Utopian communities of many kinds have been established in high confidence: when not firmly based upon religious doctrine and discipline, they nearly always dissolve before long in acrimony and mutual accusation. Communism provides us with a supreme ex-ample of this tendency in a slightly different version. It maintains itself in being, but only by means of extremely harsh repression. Let the ugliness of this not blind us to the fact that Communism started off as a seemingly *good* idea—a Utopian vision, a dream of equality and co-operation be-tween men, though with God and his law and his grace put firmly to one side. Subject to that crucial qualification, we can also say that Hitler meant well and did his best. Without the grace of God we are nothing, and worse.

Many wise monks would explain their peacefulness wholly in these terms, as something given by God, not achieved by themselves. But if we say that St. Benedict's monks are able to live together at peace because they have chosen to do so and are helped by the grace of God, will we have told the whole story? Something similar could be said, after all, of every religious order—and even, with certain qualifications, of all people who have ever tried to live the good life together, within any of the world's great religious systems and sometimes in detachment from all of them. By St. Benedict's Rule and the life of his monks, are we offered any more specific message about how peace is to be attained as between ordinary and imperfect men?

I believe that we are indeed so offered a further message of that kind, a complex and substantial and very practical one; and initially, I would like to indicate the scope and relevance which it has at the domestic level, as between people who live together in that most basic social unit of all, the family.

*   *   *

The Benedictine monastery was, from the start, conceived as a kind of family. Its monks are brothers, united in a filial relationship with their abbot—they commonly refer to themselves, collectively, as constituting the *familia* of their house.

This is their distinguishing characteristic. Before their time there were hermits, among whom, by definition, the social problem of peace did not arise. After them came the Franciscans, who originally saw themselves as a loose brotherhood of poor wayfarers, and then the Jesuits, who originally saw themselves as amounting to something rather like an army. Various human problems arose in every such case—it is never easy for men to live at peace together. But only among St. Benedict's monks were they at all closely analogous to the problems which arise within an actual worldly family; and it is to them, therefore, that the troubled family life of our time should turn if it seeks some well-tried model or lesson for secular use.

If we consider the family life of the monks in the hope of discovering the secret of its peace and stealing this for use at home, four things will strike us immediately, as contrasting sharply with certain conspicuous tendencies in the family life of our time. In the first place, we shall notice the stability already mentioned—a psychological as well as a physical stability, a strong sense of rooted permanence and belonging. In the second place, and relatedly, we shall notice that the monks appear to have resolved a conflict or dichotomy which elsewhere—in our wider social life, not only within our homes and families—generates endless trouble. However paradoxically, they contrive to live together as equals but hierarchically too—in a very real kind of freedom, but also under an unfashionably paternalistic kind of authority. The Abbot, the father of their family, is at once an absolute monarch and an equal brother, accepted without stress in both capacities, obeyed (for the most part) willingly and cheerfully but seldom corrupted by his power. Within this household, we shall find little in the way of a "generation gap," an Oedipal conflict, an unresolved dialectic of revolution and repression. (If we are family men, this negative discovery may perhaps make us feel wistfully envious.) Thirdly, we shall be struck by the physical peace of the household, its actual silence, the absence of noise. Music has a very definite place there, conversation too, even chatter and foolishness upon occasion. But we shall gather a predominant impression of the value attached to silence, the danger recognised as residing in the tongue and in all the potentialities of aggression by noise. It's seldom that a monk raises his voice; it's equally seldom that he bangs the door. And this brings us to our fourth and final observation. The absence of shouting and door-banging in this household is only one element within its tendency to be, by present-day standards, curiously ceremonious. Monks are not casual or sloppy. Towards one another, they habitually behave according to certain long-established and elaborate patterns of ritual courtesy, such as are seldom paralleled in the secular households of our time.

Apart from the grace of God, apart from the monks' general vocation to goodness and the conquest of self, these appear to me to be the four chief factors which make their family life—in the teeth of exceptional difficulties, against all human probability—so remarkably peaceful. In somewhat different versions and in varying degrees, they have done the same thing for ordinary family life at certain times and in certain societies; but among ourselves at this present time, they have very considerably ceased to do so.

Various kinds of trouble and conflict have therefore come upon the modern family; and if we had to sum these up and propose a remedy, it would be paradoxical but realistic to say that our family life has become insufficiently monastic in spirit and needs to become more so. The monks have a lesson for us, and those four elements within it deserve closer attention.

*   *   *

Generalisation has its notorious dangers. It can be agreed, none the less, that in the Western society of these last few decades, family life has become a great deal less stable than it was. The bonds within it—primarily as between husband and wife, but also as between parents and children—have been substantially weakened. The family, and even marriage itself, have come to be seen in relatively casual and temporary terms. Easy divorce means that it frequently disintegrates altogether: the practice of contraception leads to small families, and motherhood then becomes a brief interlude in a woman's life and not its main concern. The desire for greater affluence causes her to seek employment and so to devote much of her time and attention to things outside the home, while also causing her husband to work overtime or at two simultaneous jobs and so to be mostly absent, nominally for the good of the children, in practice to their psychological loss. Alternative pleasures and recreations mean that domesticity is held in low esteem, and easy transport enables all parties to get away from it. Home is still valued as the place where one sleeps (mostly) and watches television (incessantly), but it is much less widely regarded as the heart and centre, the emotional focus of life. It would not be too much to say that for some people, it has become little more than the place where one parks oneself when not in use.

The optimistic interpretation of all this is that we have achieved a degree of liberation from the stifling ties of ingrowing domesticity and can now live in a more relaxed manner, still within the family nexus, but as free equals and on a casual free-wheeling basis and independently.

But there is much sociological evidence to suggest that things are a good deal less rosy than that. There is a strong correlation, in particular, between the weakening of family ties and the rising statistics of violent crime—especially among the young—and mental breakdown.

What needs emphasis here, in contrast to that "stability" to which St. Benedict called his monks, is the instability generated by the availability and practice of easy divorce: the concept of marriage as a thing of no inherent permanence. This does not only concern those families which are actually broken up by divorce; it equally concerns those far more numerous families within which divorce is merely present as a possibility, however remote—an option for use in the last resort, a permanent qualification of the family's own permanence. To the degree that it is so regarded, a husband and wife will be less strongly motivated to make the effort needed for mutual forgiveness and domestic peace; and to that degree also, the children will grow up with a psychologically disastrous sense of insecurity. There will be no solid ground under their feet, and they will know this, even if their parents do not. Children are tensely aware of such things.

No stability, as between human beings, is ever absolute. A monk can sometimes be dispensed from his vows and so leave the cloister, and in the same sad fashion, a Christian marriage can sometimes end in legal and canonical separation. Our attempts to live at peace with one another do not always succeed.

But the harder we work at them, the more likely they are to succeed; and in family life as in the monastery, a sense of all-but-irreversible commitment will motivate us to work harder. When you are stuck with some particular group of people, peaceful relationships with them become an urgent practical necessity.

It will usually be possible, of course, to see the matter in more positive terms. For family life, St. Benedict's primary lesson concerns love and loyalty, not merely the avoidance of actual conflict. "Monastic stability implies perseverance, not only in the religious state, but also in the community in which the novice makes his religious profession. It therefore includes all the family virtues of love and loyalty known to the ancient Romans as *pietas.*" These are the virtues most sorely needed by family life today, and the monastic principle of stability is their greatest friend, the greatest friend therefore of domestic peace.

The divorce court is their greatest and most cruel enemy. You secure peace by forgiving your neighbour's faults, not by running away from them. St. Benedict was well aware of the dangers involved in any hasty headlong use of the feet.

*　　*　　*

He was equally well aware of the unfashionable fact that

shared or communal living, in a family home or a monastery, calls for authority on the one side and obedience on the other. His monks were not to live as their individual piety or fancy might dictate, but under his Rule, and—according to the provisions of that Rule—under the daily government of their abbot or father. Obedience to him was to be a primary instrument of their sanctification, and their social peace was to depend upon its careful practice.

St. Benedict learned this wisdom from the very imperfect success of monasticism in its earlier versions, during the period when it was emerging with some difficulty from origins that were eremitical and therefore, in a sense, individualistic. It was, and it still remains, a very practical kind of wisdom. But it is wisdom of a kind which our society finds highly uncongenial. The mere concepts involved in it are so very much out of favour that any mention of them is likely to trigger off a powerfully negative response, in which a neutral observer might well detect an element of neurosis. If "authority" is mentioned, a great many of us will leap at once, and most irrationally, to the conclusion that it is going to be "authoritarianism" of some arbitrary or otherwise intolerable kind; if "obedience" is mentioned, many of us will assume in the same way that this word can only refer to some abject and perhaps masochistic submission to mere blind brutal power. We seem to have rejected or forgotten the older wisdom which told us that authority (properly exercised) was a divine thing, and that obedience was "the proper office of a rational soul" and "the key to all doors." The wise men of all the world's great religions have always been aware of this twofold and most necessary principle. But to the characteristically modern mind, obsessed with the importance of each individual "doing his own thing," it seems like an absurdity or something worse.

If there is to be peace in our homes, the relationship

between children and their father will need to become a good deal more like the relationship that exists, in a good monastery, between the monks and their abbot or *abba* or father.

In other words—though this is rather a sensitive subject for a writer who is himself the father of a family—the thing needed is a certain rehabilitation of fatherhood. This is a sacred office: God himself claims no higher title than that of a father. Among men, it is still held in a certain esteem, though its biological frustration has become a personal entitlement and a major industry. But what we thus esteem is, by human and historical standards, a weak and watered-down kind of fatherhood; and we are more than likely to misinterpret the fact that Jesus told us to call God our "Father." He did. But he spoke like that in the days of the Roman *patria potestas*, when that word "father"—in daily life—stood for something much more authoritative and absolute than the vague cheque-signing benevolence which exercises a tolerant and uncertain headship in the average household of today.

The dangers of such thinking are obvious enough, and I do not wish to be understood as claiming a tyrant's role for myself and the other members of my union. Let it be agreed and asserted, therefore, that the domestic tyrant is an odious man; that obedience is sometimes given, in families and elsewhere, when it ought to be courageously withheld; and that any man in authority is in a position of great danger, morally and otherwise. My point is that St. Benedict explored this whole region very thoroughly and saw the dangers of authority no less clearly than its necessity. His abbot was to rule (in a sense) absolutely, but gently too, in consultation with others and with deep respect for the different personalities and problems of the individual monks; he was to govern not arbitrarily and according to his own whims, but within the strict unchanging framework provided by the Rule and, behind that, by the faith and morals and discipline of the Church as a whole; and he was to remember unceasingly that he was responsible not to himself, nor to those who had elected him to office, but to God, who would require a full accounting in due course. His position has been compared to that of a sea captain who is in total command while the voyage lasts, but is strictly answerable to his company as soon as the ship docks at home. St. Benedict harps upon this accountability of his almost fiercely, in words which every natural father should take most seriously to heart. His ship also will dock one day, and he also will be required to give an account of his abbatial stewardship and the souls entrusted to his care.

Temporal or fleshly fatherhood, rehabilitated on these lines and under such sanctions, would become a prime factor making for domestic peace. But for the man concerned, it would become no kind of easy promotion, no liberation of the assertive ego, no authorisation to dominate for domination's sake. It would become more of a burden, to be accepted with gratitude but very seriously and soberly, and with that sense of unworthiness—and even of fear—which any monk must feel when chosen to be abbot.

On the children's side, it would impose a corresponding burden of obedience, of deference and respect as well, a kind of social humility. We may sometimes forget that a commandment of God is here involved. "In the avalanche of more spectacular sinning which marks the end of the present stage of our civilisation, neglect of the Fourth Commandment of God passes almost unnoticed. Murder and adultery are more conspicuous than disrespect to parents." They are indeed. But you cannot break any of the Commandments, however inconspicuously, without doing major damage; and it seems clear that a vast amount of unnecessary stress and conflict and suffering is generated, within our present society, by the widespread negativism of the young towards their parents—by their sense of independence and superior wisdom, their firm resolution to "do their own thing" and on no account to seek peace and goodness of life in obedience.

But it would be tedious—and, in my view, profoundly unrealistic as well—to place the emphasis there, and so let all such considerations end up as nothing more than yet another splenetic middle-aged denunciation of the unruly young. It's far from clear that if the family life of the present day is in deep trouble, the blame lies wholly—or even chiefly—in that quarter. In connection with army life, it has been said that there are no bad soldiers but only bad officers. It could be argued, with just about the same (limited) kind of truth, that there are no bad monks but only bad abbots, and no bad children but only bad parents. The older generation, at least, would be well advised to think on these lines; and if the peace of the family breaks down, the children should not be blamed too hurriedly. Initially at least, the father should search his own conscience. How closely has he approximated to St. Benedict's ideal of the abbot? Has he been guilty (on the one hand) of tyranny or arbitrary dictatorship according to his own domineering self-will, with insufficient regard for every higher law and for each separate and sacred individuality that has been entrusted to his care? Or has he been guilty (on the other hand) of that slack easygoing permissiveness which indicates culpable indifference to what the children do and what they become?

Both possibilities are real enough. But in the present climate of opinion and social habit, the dangers of the second are greater because they can more easily pass unnoticed. The domestic tyrant and bully still exists, beyond all doubt and most destructively; the harm he does is recognised everywhere. It is less universally recognised that children have a psychological and spiritual need to grow up within some fixed frame of reference, some system of values and obligations, under gentle authority therefore and in the habit of obedience; and hence, that any failure to meet this need is going to inflict a disastrously real kind of malnutrition upon them and will be a serious failure in parental love.

The burden which St. Benedict laid upon the abbot can be seen, partly at least, as a duty of saving the brethren from that kind of malnutrition; and it lies in very much the same way upon the father of every natural human family. It's understandable, in a way, if he is reluctant to assume that burden—all burdens are burdensome. But let him at least not shrink back in revulsion from the words "authority" and "obedience," as though they stood for Hitler on the one hand and abject slavery on the other. The irrational and even neurotic nature of any such association of ideas would become apparent to him if he spent even a few days in the peace of some good monastery—an experience which any young man would be well advised to make his own in preparation for marriage, if he wanted to learn the necessary art of how to father a family in peace. In that sense among others, abbots are useful men to know and study.

St. Benedict was not primarily concerned with life in the natural human family. But he is Europe's and the world's great expert in the difficult art of being a good son and brother, and then of being a good father. We can all learn from him, to the great benefit of our family life.

*   *   *

The observant visitor to any monastery will soon come to realise that its sustained peace does indeed stem very largely from the exercise of gentle authority on the one side and the practice of willing obedience on the other. But he will notice something else a good deal sooner. At the moment of his first arrival, as the door closes behind him, his first impression will be of stillness and silence. It will be as though the closing of that door cut him off from a whole world of noise and enclosed him in a new world of quiet.

The silence of the cloister is never total. Clocks tick, bells ring from time to time, there are footsteps, never loud or hurried, always accompanied by an audible swishing of the habit; muted voices are heard from time to time, and the guest master may be positively garrulous in his concern for the visitor's comfort and convenience. There are periods, rather formidably known as "recreation," when chatter is the rule; and it must be remembered that the monks' primary task is that of *breaking* silence, of making a noise—of singing the praises of God in choir, according to that ancient and mostly psalmodic pattern of worship that we call the Divine Office.

None the less, the visitor's first and primary impression will be of silence. And if he is a sensitive man, this will strike him as something positive, not as a mere absence of noise. It will have nothing in common with the dead silence which is sometimes created, for experimental purposes, by those who wish to study the effects of sensory deprivation upon the human organism. It is something more positive than that, and even something louder. It shouts a message.

Would it seem paradoxical to suggest that the message thus shouted has a great deal in common with that conveyed by the noisy tumult of happy domesticity in a loving and united family? The contrast is obvious enough, but the similarity has struck me repeatedly. Either way, the message is the same. Silence (in the one environment) and cheerful uproar (in the other) both speak of love and peace.

But this is not the whole story. I would not rule out the possibility that monasticism may have something to learn from family life: it may well profit from that kind of experience in fact, since each monk starts off as a child in some family, and carries into the cloister whatever he has learned in that capacity. My present concern, however, is with the opposite process; and if we are considering the various senses in which St. Benedict might be regarded as the best patron for our European future, we need to remember that noisy talkative tumult, in the family and in social life generally, is not *always* a manifestation of love and peace.

The tongue is a dangerous weapon. When used too freely, when not kept under strict control, it can all too easily become an instrument for self-assertion and the domination of others; for malice and spite; for the expression—and therefore the reinforcement—of self-pity and discontent. When family peace is endangered, this is very often indeed because somebody has *said* something which never really needed to be said, and which gave offence on lines not consciously intended but perhaps not wholly unintended either.

In more general terms also, the fact is that we all talk too much. Ours is a frenetically garrulous society. In sharp contrast with the practice of earlier and simpler and less verbal peoples, we inflict upon ourselves and upon one another an endless and mostly unnecessary torrent of words—of directly spoken words in the first instance, and then of words transmitted aurally by telephone and radio, and then of words printed in newspapers and magazines and also in the continual stream of new books. We subject one another to verbal over-stimulation, which is not good for us. It is as though we were terrified of silence—of the outward silence which is broken by the spoken word, and also of the inner silence which is similarly broken by excessive random addiction to the written or printed word.

This habit of ours might be regarded as a mildly neurotic symptom, and also as a cause of personal and social stress, a thing antithetical to peace. It might be criticised at a more serious level. All the spiritual writers agree that too much talk is the enemy of the soul; and it is something else as well, as a French abbot once suggested to an English visitor. "Oui, c'est une chose merveilleuse," said the abbot. "Dans le monde hors de nos murs, on fait un grand abus de la parole." It is a serious thing to abuse speech or language or *logos*, if only because this is one of the names of God and can—since the spoken word *effects* in the hearer's mind that concept which it *signifies*—be regarded as something rather like a sacrament.

Language is a sacred thing. Those who handle it most brutally are the aggressive politicians and the aggressive advertisers, as they inflict their different kinds of violence upon us. But most of us imitate them in some degree, working thereby for stress and conflict in family life as elsewhere. But we do not need actual language for this purpose. Mere noise, involving no words at all, can have the same effect. The banging of a door can be an act of self-assertive aggressiveness, an assault upon the family's peace, and it frequently is. Something similar will often be true of any uncontrolled and inconsiderate use of the various electronic silence-shattering machines with which we of this generation tend, very significantly, to fill our homes.

"Silence" is one major part of what "peace" means. The monks have various reasons for making it into a predominant though qualified discipline of their daily lives: one of these is the fact that it helps them to hear the still small voice of God, who is easily shouted down. But another of them is the fact that it helps them to live together with a minimum of stress and conflict; and this also is a fact of relevance to family life.

*   *   *

The silence of the cloister can be regarded as one ingredient within something larger, of which the visitor will become aware at an early stage. By the standards of the present-day world outside, the life of the monks will strike him as extraordinarily ceremonious. He expected ritual, no doubt, in the abbey church, but he may be somewhat surprised by the bowings, the courtesies, the set patterns of posture and movement which he sees elsewhere; and he may be disconcerted to discover that these things are all laid down in minute detail by the written Customary of the house, and that it is one of a novice's primary tasks to master these rules and then to obey them punctiliously. What, he may ask, is the point of all this? Is it not in freedom and spontaneity that true human authenticity is to be found? Isn't there something slightly insane about a society which tells a young man—as a matter of great importance—that he must fold his arms like *this* and not like *that*, when he takes his hooded and silent place in the refectory procession? And isn't there something childish and unreal in that ritual washing of the guest's hands by the abbot, mentioned at the beginning of this book? It's certainly a "pure" ritual—that is to say, it will not make the guest's hands much cleaner if they happen to be dirty.

In countless such ways, the monks' habitual and set behaviour differs very sharply indeed from that of the outside world of today, though much less sharply from that of lay society at various times in the past. If the visitor has a narrow or provincial mind, he may be tempted to see it, initially, in psycho-pathological terms, as though monks were all organisation-fetichists. But unless he is bigoted beyond all cure, he will soon come to suspect that things are the other way round—that here, once again, it's the sane monks who have a lesson for our somewhat crazy world, and a lesson of peace.

The measured ritual or ceremony of monastic life is, initially, a matter of obedience and the silencing of self-will. By laying down the patterns of a monk's behaviour, often in very close detail, it helps him along the road to spiritual maturity by minimising the element within his life of "*I* want" and "*I* choose" and "*I* decide." But it has a further and social function as well, which can perhaps be best stated in negative terms: the casual, sloppy, spontaneous, "authentic," totally unceremonious behaviour-patterns that are so widely esteemed today are characteristically a mode of self-assertion and even of aggression, and tend steadily to make for conflict.

The fact is that Ceremony is the friend of peace, and of civilisation too. The poet Chapman was right in making that word into the name of a goddess, and in declaring her to be our prime defence against barbarism and ruin. A distinguished modern anthropologist has made very much the same point, describing ceremony or ritual as "the most potent and prevalent of social pacifiers." Most normal societies—ours is a very abnormal one—have been more or less aware of this, and have therefore attached a high social value to ritual, to courtesy, to ceremony; and it is interesting to note that military societies—armies—have done so outstandingly. Battle is a very unceremonious affair, but it isn't only in battle that soldiers tend to fight. Visitors to London may have witnessed the splendid ceremony known as The Changing of the Guard, outside Buckingham Palace. Its pattern stems from the fact that it involves the bringing together, into close proximity, of two separate bodies of armed men, the Old Guard and the New Guard, members of two different and therefore rival regiments. In the rough old days of this ceremony's first beginning, such a meeting was very likely indeed to end in violence which mere discipline would be unable to control. (As any old soldier can tell you, one's rival regiment is always far more detestable and in need of punishment than any foreign foe.) A stronger power was therefore invoked, that of the pacifier or goddess called Ceremony: the meeting of the two Guards was highly ritualised and thus rendered peaceful, and could become the colourful tourist-attraction that it now is.

This was an extreme case. The problem of maintaining peace, in the monastery or in the family, will seldom be that of restraining the physical aggressiveness of heavily-armed men who may well be imperfectly sober. But it will be a similar problem in this respect at least, that the punctilious observance of courteous and gently ceremonious behaviour-patterns will help to resolve it, while all casual sloppiness will render it more intense.

One of the three things vowed by the monk is *conversio morum* or the reformation of his own conduct. This concept and commitment reaches up to great spiritual heights. But initially, at a level which is not trivial at all, it is concerned with *moeurs* or manners, with the task of behaving courteously and respectfully toward one's neighbour, not without the aid of that powerful goddess Ceremony; and the monk's success in keeping that vow is a prime factor in establishing the distinctive peace of the cloister.

We can learn from him here: it's the well-mannered families, the courteous and even mildly ceremonious families, which are the happy and peaceful ones.

CHAPTER FOUR

I n the previous chapter, I have suggested certain lines along which a somewhat more monastic spirit and life style might help Europe to achieve social peace at the most fundamental level of all—that is to say, within the individual family. But men do not only live in families: they also live in local communities, in nations, in groups or alliances of nations, and in the human race as a world-wide whole. The problem of peace arises at each of these levels; and I now want to suggest that when we step outside the family circle and face the larger world and start to consider its social and political and international problems, we shall continue to find great practical relevance in the spirit of St. Benedict and the example of his monks.

But the first lesson we shall thereby learn is that in the very act of taking that step, we shall be switching our attention to matters of secondary importance. The monk is, by definition, a non-political animal. As I have already observed, his influence upon the larger world has been enormous and—even by purely temporal standards— enormously beneficial. But from the start, he exerted this influence indirectly, by accident as it were, and even paradoxically; in so far as he served and saved the world, he did so, initially, by turning his back on the world altogether and devoting himself to something else—to the worship of God and the seeking of goodness within a private and enclosed community. His first message to us, therefore, is that religion and family life are incomparably more important than anything which happens at the political level. That is where the quality of Europe's future is really going to be decided.

We may find this a difficult message to accept. The natural mind of our time is intensely and actively political. It instinctively sees all problems, and all possible solutions to them, in terms of government action of one kind or another. Despite the gloomy evidence provided by history and present experience, it clings to a romantically exaggerated idea of the extent to which the political process—in this preferred version or that—can by-pass the problem of individual morality and establish substantial good on its own account. It likes to "dream of systems so perfect that no one will need to be good," and it therefore concedes far more to politicians and public officials than is prudent, while expecting far more from such people than is realistic.

"Put not your trust in princes." The monk, who is something of a realist and knows his Bible, can be imagined as offering us a fairly complete political philosophy in those words. He can even be imagined as adapting a well-known pronouncement of Karl Marx and reminding us that "politics is the opium of the people." It certainly bemuses people, distracting them from the real problems of the real world. The good society can only be brought into being by the widespread and assiduous practice of individual goodness. In the idea that it can be brought closer by any exercise whatsoever of men's competitive power-lust—and that, in practice, is what the word "politics" mostly refers to—we should be able to recognise a fantasy or hallucination, such as powerful drugs can sometimes generate.

*   *   *

It still remains true that man is a social animal, necessarily involved in communities which are larger than the family and therefore in problems of the social and political kind, such as will always contain at least the possibility of conflict. What, in the concrete, can the monks teach us about "peace" at this kind of level? What changes would come upon European society if we all started to live in somewhat closer conformity with the spirit of St. Benedict?

If the monastery is a family, it is also a little kingdom, a miniature society, analogous in some ways to the larger kingdoms and societies in which the rest of us live; and as such, it will strike the visitor, paradoxically, as being both egalitarian and hierarchical, and in equally marked degree. My suggestion is that European society would do well to imitate it in both respects. Most of us already accept the egalitarian principle in one way or another. But if St. Benedict is to be our patron and guide, our understanding of that most important principle will need to be modified, and counter-balanced as well, by the complementary principle of hierarchy. If we thus contrived to make our social order somewhat more monastic, we would be going a long way towards the resolution of those class-related stresses and conflicts which—although exaggerated by the Marxists, and eagerly exacerbated by them as well—are always present and real enough and constitute a steady danger to our social peace.

It will be obvious to any casual visitor that the monks live together as equals, economically and socially too. They all wear the same habit, they eat at a common table, their possessions (which are few in number) are held more or less in common, though the rigour of this particular discipline varies from one house to another; and if one of the brethren happens to come from a noble or wealthy family, the fact will be of no interest or importance whatever to any member of the community. In the monk's life of voluntary renuncia-

tion—and, as bitter experience shows us, nowhere else—
the old vision of the Utopian Left can become a serene
reality. Theirs is truly a classless society.

It is worth remembering that they were pioneers in this
respect, historically speaking. By the monastery's sanctification of both work and poverty—two things which
had previously been held in low esteem—"it revolutionised
both the order of social values which had dominated the
slaveowning society of the Empire and that which was
expressed in the aristocratic warrior ethos of the barbarian
conquerors; so that the peasant, who for so long had been the
forgotten bearer of the whole social structure, found his way
of life recognised and honoured by the highest spiritual
authority of the age." By insisting that his monks should
work with their hands, St. Benedict did indeed establish a
social revolution, and in a sense that can be considered not
only egalitarian but "progressive" in certain other senses
too. "The monk was the first intellectual to get dirt under his
fingernails." By so doing, he not only bridged the social gulf
between the educated and governing classes (who despised
manual labour) and their slaves (who practised it), but also
the psychological gulf between the speculative and the
empirical arts; and he thereby helped to create an atmosphere in which science would become possible.

There prevails very widely today a mentality which can be
broadly defined as being democratic, progressive, and
scientific. Its sufficiency, as providing a basis for the conduct
of life, is coming to be questioned by many. But its harshest
critics will recognise wise and honourable elements within
it; and for these, St. Benedict must take much of the
historical credit.

It might be argued that if his monks preach and practise a
lesson of social equality and have done so for a long time, this
is one respect in which the modern world has nothing to

learn from them. It got the message long ago, from them and from other sources too, and is busily putting it into practice in most civilised countries if not in all. All good secular thought nowadays recognises that men are brothers and equals and must treat one another accordingly.

Such arguments would carry more weight if that dream of social equality—in its secular version—gave any promise of coming true on lines which men can be asked to tolerate. It is conceived in two equally questionable ways. Those who think on capitalistic lines conceive it mostly as equality of opportunity, with competitive avarice being then given full scope, even though the outcome is gross economic and social inequality. Those who think on socialistic lines conceive it mostly in terms of rigid social control and the envious frustration of all self-advancement outside the Party structure, even though the outcome is the grossest sort of tyranny, and poverty as well. Neither party comes realistically to terms with the fact that the only real "equality" of men is their equality before God.

A monastery, whose inhabitants live constantly and consciously in the presence of God, provides an atmosphere in which any man's claim or desire to be greater than another will be recognised at once for the absurdity which it is. It also provides an atmosphere in which both avarice and envy are known to be deadly sins, certain to doom any society which bases itself upon either of them or upon both. What replaces those two related sins, in the cloister, is a habit of detachment from economic considerations as such, and from all acquisitiveness in particular. St. Benedict recognises that even among his monks, petty economic differences will arise from time to time and may need to remain in existence. But he does not admire the "richer" monk as a great achiever, in the manner of doctrinaire capitalism; nor does he regard the "poorer" monk as suffering an outrageous injustice, in the manner of doctrinaire socialism. His approach is subtly different. Any monk who actually *needs* to have more than his brethren should recognise this fact as a weakness in himself and should therefore feel humbled or put to shame by it; and conversely, any monk whose needs are more limited ought to give thanks to God. In that respect and by God's grace, he is the more "successful" of the two.

St. Benedict thus transcends the tedious dichotomy of capitalism and socialism, offering us a third attitude towards the whole question of economics and possessions and one's "standard of living"—an attitude which, in so far as it might become more widely adopted, would do great things for the cause of social peace, resolving those tensions which are now so very imperfectly resolved by our political strivings after "equality." He proposes a new perspective. Let us imagine some man who cannot see without glasses or walk without a stick. In charity, we shall want him to have those things. But we shall recognise his dependence upon them as a weakness and a misfortune—we shall not admire him for possessing them, nor shall we consider it unjust that he should possess them when others do not. St. Benedict's implied suggestion is that we should look in much the same way upon any man who depends, for the kind of happiness or fulfilment which he has in mind, upon a whole variety of such expensive things as big cars, lavish meals, non-stop electronic entertainment, social splendours, colourful holidays abroad, and political power. None of these things is bad in itself. But a man who depends upon them for his sense of well-being is neither to be admired as a success nor hated as an enemy of the people; in his dependence, he is above all to be *pitied* just as you and I would naturally pity the near-blind, near-crippled condition of that other man. He is a weak man, a failure.

*   *   *

Inequality, when considered as a danger to social peace, does not have to be economic. Differences of class and education and culture can generate quite as much stress as differences in wealth, and many people are far more destructively anxious about their exact status, their position in the pecking-order, than by any question of money or possessions or standard of living.

In this respect, one might suppose that a perfect human society—supposing that such a thing could exist—would be utterly egalitarian, with no class-system or pecking-order whatsoever, no remotest possibility of snobbery in any version. A Christian might perhaps have his doubts about this. His faith has spoken much of the genuinely perfect society—namely, that of Heaven—and has shown a consistent tendency to see it in hierarchical terms. But in this life, the question is a shade academic. No human society, not even that of a monastery, is going to be perfect; even here in the cloister questions of position and status and precedence are going to arise and demand some kind of response.

Human nature being what it is, there are—in the monastery's version of this problem, and in Europe's as well—only two real options. On the one hand, each individual's status or seniority can be defined, once and for all, so as to constitute a kind of fixed *datum* in his life and his relationships with others. On the other hand, all such questions can be caused to remain permanently open, permanently fluid and flexible, so that each individual's place in the social "pecking-order" will be determined by his own behaviour and subject to constant readjustment throughout his life.

St. Benedict was a realist, and it was his concern "to settle, with precision and finality, all external matters which could possibly become a cause of distraction, or disturb the monastic peace." He therefore opted firmly for the first of these two alternatives, knowing perfectly well that where men's status is undefined or uncertain, it tends very strongly to become the object of their habitual preoccupation and anxiety, of contention and bickering, of endless quasi-political competition. Anything of that kind would endanger the peace of the cloister, while distracting the brethren from more important matters. He decreed, therefore, that each monk's status or position was to be simply a matter of his seniority or age—not his age as a man, but his age as a monk. The date of his entry into the community was to settle the question absolutely. He did not thereby eliminate "social mobility" altogether, since every junior monk would naturally become a senior monk in the course of time. But he prevented it from becoming a matter of uncertainty and therefore of contention. He was concerned with peace.

It will not be denied that St. Benedict's decision in this matter was profoundly alien to the spirit of our own time. For most of us, the concepts of "democracy" and "equality" and "freedom" dictate a highly positive attitude towards social mobility. In any suggestion that it might be a good thing for a man to have his place within the social hierarchy, to know what it is and be satisfied with it, we are naturally disposed to see nothing but the arrogance of privilege. Let the lower classes be content with that humble position to which it has pleased God to call them! Let them not get fancy ideas! Then we, the rich and powerful, will be able to enjoy ourselves irresponsibly, without fear of revolutionary challenge.

On such lines, most men of our time will react at once—and angrily—against any recommendation of an established and hierarchical social order. They will have perceived a certain manifest truth. But they will not have perceived the *whole* truth. There is a social and moral case for hierarchy, and even for an aristocracy of birth. Absolute social equality seems to be unattainable, outside certain small tribal communities of the hunting-and-gathering sort. In any European future that we can imagine, some people are going to be top-dogs while others—much more numerous—are going to be under-dogs in some degree. Given this probably inescapable fact, do we *want* its practical working-out to be a matter of incessant contention? And do we *want* our top-dogs, the members of our social elite at its various levels, to be men of the thrustingly competitive kind, rat-race winners by talent and temperament? "Aristocrats"—of one kind or another—we shall certainly have. By what process do we want them to be chosen? By their avarice, their commercial success, their wealth? By their standing in the villainous Party? It's arguable, to say the least, that we would do better—and even act more democratically—if we chose them by lottery from among the ordinary run of men, and even by the supreme lottery of birth, in which chance (which some call the finger of God) operates absolutely.

One thing is clear at least. Aristocracies of birth have been guilty, throughout our European past, of countless moral and social atrocities—though the alternative aristocracies, of money and (especially) of Nazi or revolutionary or Communist ideology, have done no better. But the proud nobleman did at least enrich our culture. Travel throughout the length and breadth of Europe, and consider those buildings and artefacts which cause the modern tourist to gape in astonishment, as at some great splendour now lost and unattainable. Behind each of them, if you look in the guide-book, you will usually detect the power and patronage of some man who was—by the standards of the too-simply democratic mind—wholly deplorable: some King or Emperor, some rich baron, some arrogant Prince-Bishop. Then, by contrast, look at what the aristocracies of money and ideology have produced!

Man does not live by standard-of-living alone.

The democratic or egalitarian principle is a profound truth about ourselves and a necessary element within the make-up of any tolerable society. It has its clear place in the Rule of St. Benedict and in the monastic life. But unless complemented or counter-balanced by the opposite principle of stable hierarchy, it erects envy and contention into a way of life—a fact to which the present state of England and of Europe bears ample witness.

It also generates psychological stress. A social order which is more or less fixed, more or less hierarchical, does set limits to the social and economic ambitions of the individual. But these are limited in any case, since only a few of us can rise to the top; and if fixity of status is a restrictive thing in one sense, it is a supportive thing in another. Men do have economic needs. But once these are met at a fairly basic level, they have psychological needs which matter to them a great deal more. And among these is the need to have an identity, a place in the world, a sense of *belonging* somewhere. In a feudally structured society, a humble man could know where, and to whom, he belonged. He could gather a kind of strength from saying to himself, "I am my Lord of Barchester's man," no matter how grossly imperfect a man my Lord of Barchester might be. (In the Anglo-Saxon poem called *The Wanderer*, it is reckoned as the worst of temporal misfortunes for a man to be without a lord.) The fluid and unstructured societies of today offer various benefits to their citizens, but no version at all of this particular benefit, which is an important one. They make the individual "free," but at the cost of reducing him to a rootless and atomic personnel-unit. He can go here or he can go there, he can become richer or poorer, he can embark upon voluntary relationships with this individual or that group and terminate these when he sees fit. But he doesn't really *belong* anywhere at all; and a great many of our social tensions and conflicts stem directly from a universal but dim awareness of that intolerable deprivation.

The concept of having and knowing one's place in the world deserves a certain rehabilitation. More is involved here than mere abject servility before one's supposed betters.

*　　*　　*

I have been suggesting that St. Benedict's monks offer a most useful pattern for the social peace of our European future, in the first place by constituting an equal or democratic society in a deep sense which excludes envious contention, and then by constituting a society which is also hierarchical and ordered, and peaceful for that reason. We shall do well to learn the implied lesson.

But we shall also do well to consider the notion of "government" that prevails in the monastery, and reconsider our notion of secular government in the light of what we there discover.

All the world knows that a monastery is governed by its abbot. Theologically speaking, no man need suffer the misfortune of being without a Lord. But every monk has a "lord" in the more direct and human sense, to whom his allegiance is pledged in an almost feudal manner, and he thereby gains psychological support of the kind already mentioned. He also comes under authority thereby, a kind of government, and the nature of this deserves attention.

It does not—as far as I can see—cast very much light upon

the political and governmental problems of the world outside, if we understand these in terms of one *kind* of government as against another. It certainly embodies (and thereby endorses) the democratic principle, since St. Benedict wants the abbot to be elected by the community he is to rule, unanimously if possible. But it qualifies that principle, since the Rule is careful not to give absolute rights to the majority and allows for outside intervention in bad cases; and it also embodies the authoritarian or monarchical principle, since the abbot—when duly elected and enthroned—exercises his authority on more or less absolute lines.

St. Benedict was naturally aware of the dangers that would therefore arise, and he offers lengthy recommendations as to what kind of man ought to be chosen as abbot. But these, although interesting, are somewhat platitudinous. They tell us little more than that the abbot needs to be a very *good* man, with the particular human qualities that characterise the good father of any family or the good ruler of any country.

It might seem, therefore, that the monks have little light to cast upon our political problems outside the cloister. Their Rule offers *some* degree of endorsement to any system that we are likely to propose, while endorsing none without qualification. It therefore leaves our actual arguments very much where they were; nor does it help us much to be told that rulers ought to be very good men. We always knew that. The whole problem arises because bad men desire power over others—in politics and elsewhere—very much more passionately than good men do, and pursue it very much more unscrupulously, and therefore tend to be the ones who actually secure it.

But the picture changes if we stop thinking about alternative systems, and turn our attention instead to the kind of thing that "government" is in general, to the manner in which it is conceived within the cloister and in the present-day world elsewhere. We shall then find a sharp twofold contrast. In the abbot's rule and the government of the house in general, the monks see something *sacred* and therefore something *limited*. It is our instinct to look upon secular government in wholly secular and profane and functional terms and—perhaps for that reason—to set no limits to it.

Here also, and in both respects, we have something to learn.

* * *

What kind of picture comes into your mind when you consider the words "a government building"?

Our society being what it is, the first thing suggested to you by those words will probably be a large modern structure, all steel and concrete and glass, full of administrators and secretaries and filing cabinets and computers, so designed as to enable the business of the State to be carried on as efficiently as possible. Such an understanding of the words will stem naturally from our dominant present-day assumptions about what "government" is, and about what can properly be regarded as its prime business.

But those assumptions of ours have not been held always and by all men, as we can see at once by considering the Palace of Versailles. This was undoubtedly conceived from the start as "a government building," but according to a very different and primarily *ceremonial* notion of what "government" is. If conceived as the functional headquarters of an administration, it was always grossly inefficient and generally unsuitable. But it was never so conceived. It was built—ruinously, so far as the French people were concerned—to serve as a worthy temple in which the divine ritual of kingship could be fittingly enacted. The assumption behind it is one that will seem merely absurd to anyone whose mind works on functionally and economically political lines, but has none the less come naturally to most human societies at most periods in history. It is what Confucius had in mind when he said that "Ceremonies are the first thing to be attended to in the practice of government." It is what causes most "primitive" peoples to conceive their kings and rulers in more or less priestly terms. It is what led certain mediaeval theologians to believe that the coronation of a king was actually a sacrament. It is what causes the English people to accord to their vestigial Monarchy, and to all the associated splendour of ceremonial, a veneration which they firmly and rightly withhold from their politicians and bureaucrats.

This is a very deep-seated human instinct. It amounts to a recognition that government is an essentially *sacred* thing; that all human authority comes from God; that any king or other ruler enacts a God-like role among men, his power being an ectype or derivative of the Divine omnipotence. It is an instinct or perception that makes for peace, and its very deep frustration, in the troubled societies of today, provides us with yet another reason for taking seriously the example set to us by the monks.

When a present-day abbot invites you into his room, you will probably find a telephone there, a typewriter, even a filing cabinet. The circumstances of the time mean that some of his work resembles that of a manager or bureaucrat and has to be done on the same drab lines. But when so occupied, he is being the servant of the community rather than its *abba* or father. To see him at his most abbatial, wait for some big feast day and attend his Solemn Pontifical High Mass, at which—by long tradition—he will preside in the full stately *pontificalia* of a bishop, though he is unlikely to hold that sacramental dignity in fact. So vested, he will be enacting the role of Christ among his disciples, while also symbolising—in his own person—the life and unity of the abbey. His office is not *wholly* ceremonial in nature. But it has that character initially, fundamentally—everything else about him stems from that aspect of it, as from a starting-point.

One of the things that stem from it is the distinctive monastic concept of duly constituted authority, of law, and of obedience; and here again, there is a lesson for our secular existence and our hope of peace.

You and I probably obey the civil law, broadly at least, though perhaps with occasional lapses. We do so partly for merely prudential reasons. We know that if we break the law substantially and are found out, we shall probably go to jail. But we also have a certain social conscience in this matter. We know that if each individual feels free to break the generally-accepted rules, life is going to become a great deal more difficult and unpleasant for one and all. And even where no such danger of anarchy is directly involved, we feel that it's somehow *wrong* to break the law.

None the less, we have a deep-seated instinct to regard ourselves as being, in the last resort, the originators and masters and manipulators of the law. Governments make the law, but they do so as delegates of the people and are answerable to them. They derive their authority from nothing higher than ourselves, and they can expect to be voted out of office—or, perhaps, overthrown by revolution—if they flout the popular will too grievously.

Assumptions of this kind lie behind practically all secular government of the present day, not only when it is of the "democratic" sort. They are set forth explicitly in the Declaration of Independence, from which the American Constitution takes its origin. But in very much the same way, a Soviet theorist will tell you that the Party embodies the will of the people. Even Hitler claimed that the spirit and will of the German *volk* was incarnate and operative in his own person.

The monks see things differently. They know that the abbot was elected by themselves from among their number, and that one part of his liturgical role is that of enacting the identity and common life of the community. But they do not regard his authority as having the secular or popular character of being derived from themselves. They see it as coming directly from God, and in fact as *being* the delegated authority of God, so that obedience to him becomes a fully religious act and duty and privilege. It does of course help to maintain the domestic peace of the monastery, and this is important at one rock-bottom level; it does of course provide ample scope for the renunciation of self-will, and this is important at a much deeper level. Beyond this, if the community is in a healthy condition, the rule of the abbot will normally coincide with its collective purpose or intention, and will then correspond—in a certain sense— with "the will of the people."

But even then, it will not be obeyed *for that reason*. The abbot's authority comes from God, and he is answerable only to God for his use of it. It is a sacred thing, and is revered and obeyed as such.

It would make for peace, and for temporal well-being in general, if we started to look on secular government in the same light, instead of trying to believe that it somehow embodied and implemented "the will of the people." This was always an unrealistic idea, if only because there is no such thing as "the will of the people." There are a great many people, and they all have different wills—different interests, different passions and prejudices as well, coinciding here and there so as to generate some limited and temporary *consensus*, but never very consistently or ascertainably. The opinion-polls tell us something about their ever-changing patterns, but not very much; elections tell us even less, and when the victorious politicians claim thereafter to embody the people's will, they lie.

The fact is that government by "the will of the people" is a fiction or fantasy, except in so far as government is prepared to go out of business altogether and leave each individual to follow his own will absolutely—an idea which has its attractions in theory, but would prove impossibly anarchic in practice. What we get, when we seek to enthrone the popular will, is government by contention—the temporary enthronement of those who emerge as the victors in some kind of electoral and parliamentary rat-race, and who then reign until torn down by other and stronger rats. Our daily newspapers illustrate this fact with depressing clarity.

If we care about peace, therefore, we might do well to reappraise the Benedictine concept of government by the will of God. Unlike the "will of the people," this actually exists and can be ascertained, sufficiently at least, and is stable and unchanging; and it is the only thing that can possibly guarantee long-term justice. The rulers, when regarded as answerable only to the people, can "get away with murder"—always in the figurative sense, and often literally. But there is one Supreme Court that cannot be fooled. Abbots live in daily fear of it. The future and the peace of Europe would look more promising if the same could be said of our secular rulers. There are worse things to lose than elections.

*   *   *

The above considerations might seem to point towards a concept of government which most of us would reject violently as being arrogantly ostentatious and harshly authoritarian. But within the cloister at least, it doesn't work out like that. There have been bad abbots in the past, proud and tyrannical. There are probably some today. But they have always been exceptional. Most abbots are humble men, and rule gently.

This is partly because they started off as mere monks, their characters being modified accordingly. But it is also because the very sacredness of their rule makes it into a distinctly limited thing, circumscribing their actions, inhibiting any random self-assertive use of their authority.

The point is that anything recognised as sacred is naturally regarded as calling for carefully disciplined handling. Men are only casual or permissive about those things which they regard as trivial. In our profoundly Manichaean culture, a great many people regard sex as something trivial if not worse, and are therefore thoroughly permissive about its handling. But those who take a higher view of it naturally regard it as something which must always be hedged around with rules and restrictions which will seem repressive at times—not because it is evil, but because it is momentous and holy and therefore open to serious abuse. It is indeed momentous, sacred as well. The husband who lawfully begets a baby upon his wife is not merely scratching a bodily itch. He is doing something which has its roots in the Godhead. He is enacting—at the human level—the union in God of love and creativity, and also the fertile union between Christ and his Church. But from the sacramental greatness and holiness of sex as so conceived, it does *not* follow that all sexual behaviour is automatically good. Very much the reverse.

Something similar is true of any exercise of temporal power. This also has its roots in the Godhead, as the Lord observed to Pilate: kings and other rulers do exercise a priestly and even God-like role among men, and are rightly looked upon with a certain awe. But this fact does *not* give them any privilege of acting permissively, as though anything they choose to do would automatically be right and proper and deserving of the citizens' obedience. Very much the reverse. A high degree of self-discipline is called for, as in that other matter. Sex is good, but the kind of sexual behaviour which comes most naturally or instinctively to fallen men is decidedly evil. The exercise of temporal authority is good, but when fallen men find themselves in positions of temporal authority, the kind of behaviour which comes most naturally or instinctively to them is very nasty indeed.

My subject is the future of Europe, and of its peace; and if this peace is to be maintained at the national and political level, it is not enough to say that citizens ought to obey the law. The law itself must also deserve that name and be such that the citizens can decently be asked to obey it. In my own country at least, a long period of what might be called "political permissiveness" has led to a very different situation—one in which a large proportion of what passes for "law" is in fact little more than the organised impudence of politicians and bureaucrats, and deserves no respect or obedience at all. This situation has developed steadily over the years, ever since we first separated the idea of government from the idea of holiness, and therefore from any possible idea of Natural Law or Justice—without which, as St. Augustine observed, the government becomes indistinguishable from the Mafia. And as government came to be seen as something secular or profane, it also and inevitably came to be seen as something unlimited, wholly free to legislate as it chose and naturally engaged in incessant legislation, with the courts enforcing its arbitrary will at every point. We thus departed radically from the view of government which was taken by Aristotle, Aquinas,

Bracton, Hooker, and Grotius, and by other such champions of the English Common Law as, for example, the great Sir Edward Coke. For these authorities, as for Christian and civilised men in general, "law" was always a datum, never an activity. It was something which created the government and circumscribed its authority, never something which the government created.

But we English are not the only people to follow this ugly path, which leads naturally and logically to totalitarianism. It has been trodden, in varying degrees, by all Europe.

The Benedictine abbot here provides us with a model for secular adoption, in the interests of justice and therefore of peace. He does not and cannot rule permissively—his authority is sacred, and is therefore limited. He administers, he governs, he can even punish, but he hardly legislates at all. When he takes office, he finds a full framework of established law already in existence and operative. This is provided primarily by the Catholic Faith itself and the Canon Law of the Church, and then by the Rule, and finally by the Constitution or Customary of the particular abbey in question. The latter will need modification from time to time, but only within the settled framework of those wider structures and with the assent of those concerned.

Like the captain of a ship, the abbot is—in certain senses, and for a limited time—an absolute monarch. Liturgically speaking, he enacts that role with some splendour. But if any man's power-lust causes him to dream of becoming an absolute monarch, of dominating others by the capricious exercise of his own will, of laying down the law according to his own arbitrary notions, he should not aspire to be an abbot. Such a man would find that particular monarchy a deeply frustrating one; and in fact, of course, he would never be elected to it. A political candidate can easily conceal the fact of his power-lust from the electorate, and frequently does. A monk, having that fault, will hardly be able to conceal it from the brethren with whom he has lived in close contact for many years.

It is an ugly fault, a highly destructive lust. "La fureur de dominer," said Voltaire, "est de toutes les maladies de l'esprit humain la plus terrible." Against that sickness, the Rule of St. Benedict acts as a most powerful medicine; and this is one prime reason why monasteries are such peaceful places.

*   *   *

The peace of Europe depends upon the re-establishment of order, and therefore upon a certain rehabilitation of "authority"—a concept which has been much abused in our recent past and has fallen into undeserved disrepute. It is something that we need—in the family, in the State, and in all the various intermediate structures and organisations within which we live and work. At every such level, it certainly does call, on the one side, for the unpopular virtue of obedience. But it also calls, on the other side and perhaps even more crucially, for a renewed sense of self-discipline, of subordination to a higher Law, and of responsibility to God rather than to man. Unless so governed, authority becomes the authoritarianism or tyranny which men rightly detest.

In this respect, the monks offer us a lesson and a model. But they also do so in another respect which deserves attention.

We all hope for peace within the nation. But we also hope for peace as between different nations; and here, Europe's past record is no great matter for pride. In the hope of improving upon it, many people are working towards a certain pooling of national identities into what might eventually become a Federation or a United States of Europe, a super-power perhaps, and one within which war between, say, France and Germany would be just as unlikely as a present-day war between, say, Massachusetts and South Carolina.

A cynic will observe that despite the existence of just such a federal system, Massachusetts and South Carolina *were* at war not much more than a century ago. Even so, aspirations of that kind have a great deal to commend them. A fully united Europe, with a common citizenship and a common currency, is probably an unworkable ideal unless a common Faith supports it, but it is at least not an ignoble ideal.

But it is an ideal which needs to be counter-balanced by today's very strong and understandable tendency towards decentralisation and local autonomy, and partly for the sake of peace. Wars have many causes. One factor which frequently tends to trigger them off is the irritated impatience felt by those who find themselves governed by strangers from afar. "Why can't we be allowed to manage our own lives?" they ask; and it was this feeling, quite as much as the desire to retain slavery, which prompted the American Confederacy to secede from the Union.

Local autonomy does not make for peace infallibly. Throughout history, it has been no rare thing for small nations—and even small city-states—to start fighting one another. But at the worst, they have then embarked upon necessarily small wars. It takes great empires and super-powers to achieve the spectacular kind of carnage in which our century has specialised so efficiently.

In this respect, the Benedictine abbey stands for a principle which needs to be safeguarded. Within the Church, certain religious orders have been somewhat analogous to great empires or super-powers, monolithically run, tightly disciplined from the centre. By contrast, St. Benedict envisaged each monastery as something rather like a tiny city-state, a wholly autonomous community, self-sufficient in so far as this was locally possible. Later developments modified this concept in some degree: the Cluniac reform made for a more unified "Order" of St. Benedict, and Pope Leo XIII took this a stage further in 1893, establishing an Abbot Primate in Rome to be the general father of all monks everywhere. But he was never meant to be anything like the General of an army or of the Jesuits, a central commander. Individual self-governing monasteries, loosely federated into a number of different "congregations," are still the primary units of monastic living.

Europe might do well to model its political future on analogous lines. As a brotherhood of peoples, loosely federated but with much regional and local autonomy, it can hope to live without too much of the stress which generates conflict. But there will inevitably be pressures tending to make it into a rigidly centralised tyranny of the "Eurocrats" in Brussels, and these will need to be resisted. Otherwise, the omens for long-term peace will be bad.

*   *   *

The most obvious antithesis to peace is war—actual fighting, actual bloodshed and killing. There has been far too much of this in Europe's past, and far too much easy justification of it in Christ's name. This is one reason why I propose the monk—rather than the Crusader or the Grand Inquisitor—as the right pattern or paradigm for our future. Far too often, we have tried to do the work of Jesus by the methods of those who crucified him, and have thus—not very surprisingly—caused the Church to be hated and feared instead of being loved and trusted. Far too often, we have forgotten that the "Holy War" is emphatically a Moslem rather than a Christian concept. In our language, that phrase is almost a contradiction in terms. A war can occasionally be "just," in the sense of being morally defensible despite its inherent hatefulness. It can never be "holy," in any sense that would imply a possibility of actually pleasing God by killing his children. (You certainly cannot please me by killing my children, though I can imagine circumstances that would make it easier for me to forgive you if you did; and is God a less devoted father than I am?)

The monks are able to be men of peace, partly because they are heavily armed with two of the most powerful weapons in existence—namely, prayer and penance. Those of us who trust in weaker and dirtier weapons commonly fail in the very measure of their success. It is ironical (for example) to remember the motivations which led us, here in England, to declare war in 1939. In general, we wanted to save Europe from being overshadowed and partly occupied by a cruel totalitarian and militant tyranny. In particular, we wanted to protect the freedom and the territorial integrity of Poland. We certainly "won" that war, or were on the winning side at least. But did we achieve either of those two objectives?

The monk's victories are more substantial.

He plainly offers us an example of gentleness, of non-violence; and if we all started to live with a little more of his restraint and abstemiousness, the danger of war would grow substantially less. Not all the causes of war are economic, but some of them are, and competitive greed does not make for peace.

The cultivation and expansion of needs is the antithesis of wisdom. Every increase of needs tends to increase one's dependence on outside forces over which one cannot have control, and therefore increases existential fear. Only by a reduction of needs can one promote a genuine reduction in those tensions which are the ultimate causes of strife and war.

If we lived a little more monastically, we would live a great deal more peacefully.

We, here in Europe, may not need the monks to tell us to refrain from aggressive wars and fighting among ourselves. But what if we are attacked from the outside? Have the monks got anything to say about the agonising problem of Europe's defence against the aggressive and atheistic power of Soviet Communism?

It is indeed an agonising problem, a dilemma. Nations, in general, have a right to defend themselves against unjust aggression. Christendom (in so far as such a thing still exists) has a further right to defend itself against forcibly-imposed infidelity or atheism. On the other hand, recent technological developments have been such as to make it practically certain that any major war, in our time, is going to be waged by methods so indiscriminately destructive and even so genocidal as to be clearly immoral, while making any possible "victory" into a tragic and empty thing indeed. No kind of end can justify so blatantly wicked a means. On the other hand again, it seems absurd and even indecent to suggest that it might be our duty to hand Europe over to the Russian Communists, humbly and on a plate, whenever they choose to ask for it with sufficient ferocity.

We can blame the scientists for this dilemma. By making the "just war" into a practical impossibility, their clever inventions have added enormously to the temporal power of the unscrupulous over those who seek to obey the law of God.

It is a moral dilemma, and it has been discussed very widely. It cannot be pursued here at any depth, but nor can it be simply passed over in a book concerned primarily with peace. The monks, as such, can perhaps be regarded as making three contributions to it. In the first place, they remind us to be men of peace. Any positive hawkishness or bellicosity or blood-lust is to be ruled out absolutely—one may sometimes need to fight, but always reluctantly. Then, their life of penance should remind us that every Christian is called, in principle, to martyrdom. He has no business to make his own temporal well-being, or even the preservation of his own life, into an absolute. But thirdly, he can console us by the "extaordinary recuperative power" of the monastic institution, especially as illustrated during its earlier centuries. Monks are easy to kill, as good men always must be: Jesus gave the Roman soldiers no trouble. But like him, they show a tremendous ability to come bouncing back in full life and power; and if the worst came to the worst, a Europe that lived by their spirit and his might best confound its enemies by displaying that same talent for resurrection.

* * *

One final point remains. When we think of living at peace with our neighbours, we are all too likely to forget the importance of living at peace with our *dead* neighbours. It is true that if we fight them, they are in no position to fight back. But when seen timelessly and in the perspective provided by the Communion of Saints—which is how a good monk sees all things—they turn out to be our fellow creatures and fellow citizens, our fellow voters even, having their own wisdom which will certainly be limited, but which will, none the less, be able to supplement the limitations of our own. They may well have been foolish and wicked in their day and in their degree. But their faults and follies will have been different from our own, and will therefore have a kind of corrective usefulness at least.

If the monastery lives at peace, it does so largely by attaching a high value to continuity and tradition. There is always need for change and reform, and even, in certain senses, for revolution. This is true within the Church itself, though the wild excesses of these last few years—manifestations, perhaps, of post-Conciliar trauma—may perhaps tend to conceal this fact from sober and responsible eyes. But the monk's vocation was never of this kind. Others may perhaps be called to "progressiveness" in thought and action; he is called to peace and stability, to an outlook and mentality and life style that are deeply rooted in the centuries and attach little value to change, and he has no sympathy at all with the Oedipal or Jacobin urge which makes men desire to break sharply away from their past and their inheritance.

In this respect, he stands for one side only of a complex truth. But he stands for the side of it which needs the strongest emphasis today. For Europe and for the Church as well, his message is that any sudden violent break with the past is certain to prove destructive and barbarising. It will be an act of aggressiveness, of hatred; and the monk is a man of peace.

CHAPTER FIVE

Peace be with you! It was in these traditional words that the risen Jesus greeted his disciples, and they are echoed in the liturgical greeting of any Catholic bishop, representative of Jesus, to a gathered congregation. What do they mean?

In our time, the word "peace" has come to have an unfortunately narrow or specialised usage, as though it referred primarily, or even *only*, to an absence or non-existence of armed conflict. This is an important sense of the word, but a negative and secondary one. The risen Jesus did not want his disciples to fight among themselves; the modern bishop, if you asked him, would certainly express a desire that his flock should be spared the horrors of World War III. But this sense of the word, although desperately important at its own level, is not the primary concern of that ancient greeting, which goes deeper.

Like any conventional greeting, it can be emptied of all genuine content by casual repetition. When one good Jew greets another with "shalom aleichem," he may mean nothing more specific than an Englishman's "How do you do?" which is certainly not a request for information. But circumstances may sometimes bring it to new life. Imagine that you have just seen your best friend and beloved master beaten up and tortured to death by the cops, and the battered bloodstained corpse then taken away and buried. Now, just a day or two later, that same friend and master is suddenly with you once again, in the room with you and your friends, alive and well. What is he going to say? What will he *need* to say? You are all traumatised, flattened, shattered by this unbelievable fact of his reappearance: it generates an intolerable tension and conflict between your eyes and your minds, your familiar world has collapsed, a pit of madness seems to be opening up at your feet. If your friend, noticing this situation, were then to say "Peace be with you!" his primary meaning might be very like what an American has in mind when he says to another citizen of that tensed-up country "Relax!"

It is part of the Christian message, repeatedly emphasised in the Gospels, that men *should* relax—not in the sense of abandoning all effort and drifting with the tide, but in the sense of freeing themselves from anxiety and inner conflict and trusting in the Lord; and here we come much closer to the heart of what "peace" means—the "shalom" of the Jews, the "salaam" of the Moslems, and even "Islam." These three words are closely related; and the third, being the name of a traditionally militant faith, can hardly be understood as meaning "peace" in the primary modern sense. (If we needed to translate it, we might do well to take over the title of a certain classic of Jesuit spirituality, and say that "Islam" means "abandonment to the Divine Providence.")

On such lines as these, we can approach a third sense in which the Rule and spirit and tradition of St. Benedict, if made our own, could be of enormous practical value for the future of Europe and that of the West in general. We need to live at peace with the natural world around us, and also with other men and women, our neighbours. If we fail to do so, our temporal well-being and even our survival will be at risk. But each one of us also faces the possibly harder task of living at peace with himself; and this kind of peace is perhaps the most important of all, as being a precondition of those other two kinds. Violent and aggressive behaviour towards the non-human creation or towards other people very commonly stems from the fact that the person concerned is projecting upon the outside world some unresolved tension or conflict within himself.

How very much less unpleasant the recent history of Europe would have been, if only Hitler had been a relaxed and easy-going kind of man!

*   *   *

It has never been altogether easy for men to relax and be at peace with themselves. But is there any sense in which this is an exceptionally serious problem for the men of our time? In this respect, were things easier in the Good Old Days?

Obviously they were!—or so, at least, some voice or instinct within us is tempted to reply. But then, another voice or instinct speaks within us, saying that any sweeping judgment of that kind is bound to be an illusion of perspective. Neither voice, neither instinct is to be trusted entirely.

The difficulty of the question needs to be recognised. It is never easy to make any kind of reliably objective comparison between the life and experience of one's own time and that of the past, or of any particular period within the past. The very immediacy of the present, coupled with the uncertainty of its future, gives it an anxious or urgent quality which the absent past—with its settled and known outcomes—can never have. The two cannot possibly present themselves to one's consciousness, for purposes of comparison, on anything like equal terms. And in our time, any such comparison has become exceptionally difficult, simply because so much more gets onto the record now than ever before. Countless things get printed and taped and filmed nowadays, so becoming known to all of us, which at any previous period would have sunk without trace, disappearing into "the dark backward and abysm of time" and leaving no mark of their brief urgency except in the short-term memory of those directly concerned.

So we need to be very careful when we attribute any distinctive character, whether good or bad, to the life and society of our own time as against that of the past. To a degree that cannot be assessed, the difference may lie in the extent of our knowledge rather than in the realities under discussion. It is easy—and even, in a curious way, agreeable—to speak of

> this strange disease of modern life
> With its sick hurry, its divided aims,
> Its heads o'ertaxed, its palsied hearts,

its pressures and turmoils and anxieties, as though life were altogether simple and relaxed in the Good Old Days, before things started to become complicated and tense. We cannot look into the minds of the dead, but things probably weren't "simple and relaxed in the Good Old Days." Symptoms of tension and despair—such as mindless violence, and the use of drugs, and madness, and suicide—are displayed by most societies of which we have any record, if not by all. A very large proportion of history's grand crucial events, when considered with any cool detached objectivity, suggest the behaviour of people whom extreme stress has pushed to the borderline of sanity, or beyond it. If you and I are churned up by internal stresses and lunacies, we aren't the first. Men have always found that "peace"—in the primary sense of *shalom* or internal serenity, and then and therefore in other senses—is a painfully elusive thing. Perhaps this is because they haven't always been looking for it so very seriously, being distracted from it by the rival charms of self-love and self-assertion. The problem of living at peace with oneself is not peculiar to this generation, and we cannot even be sure that our experience of it is exceptionally intense.

But we can be sure of one thing: quite clearly, this is not one of those numerous problems which have been solved, more or less completely, by scientific and technological developments and by the affluence which has stemmed from them. We have certainly found ways of making it less agonising. Alcohol and tobacco and hashish and caffeine have been available for a long time, and have been very extensively used in order to modify consciousness by chemical means and so make the burden of self less intolerable. There are now more sophisticated drugs, able to do that same task a good deal more efficiently, so that tranquillisers are consumed on a colossal scale throughout the modern West, while some of our younger people have established a whole life style—almost an ideology—upon the pursuit of chemical hallucination. But all these things only palliate the symptoms, and their popularity makes it clear that the disease is an extremely prevalent one today, however rare or widespread it may have been in the past: for all his ingenuity, modern man has not yet worked out an effective technique for solving this problem.

His attempts to do so—by non-chemical means, that is— are broadly of two kinds, easily distinguished in theory. On the one hand, there is what may be called the medical approach. Every doctor knows that psychological stress can damage the body, and its relief is therefore his concern; it is our instinct to see psychoanalysis and every kind of psychiatry as one specialised branch of the medical profession and the medical task. On the other hand, there is the religious approach; and it is our instinct to see the priest, or parson, or rabbi, or guru, or shaman as a man very unlike the doctor, engaged in a very different task. But this distinction is less clear-cut than it seems. It has often been pointed out, for example, that psychoanalysis, when considered in terms of social anthropology, functions very much like a religion—having its priesthood and its contentious dogmatisms and its heresy-hunts, and even something analogous to an Apostolic Succession. Conversely, very much of what we instinctively label as "religion" turns out, upon closer examination, to be (perhaps partially, perhaps completely) one version or another of psychosomatic relaxation, ordered chiefly or solely to the individual's tranquillity or inward peace and therefore to his bodily health as well.

In our present context, this latter point needs some further development. It seems to be very largely true, for example, of various quasi-religious cults or practices which have become popular in our time, such as Transcendental Meditation or Zen. I intend no disparagement of these practices when I say that they achieve, at a profound level, what is achieved clumsily and superficially by a tranquilliser: they enable the troubled individual to resolve his inner conflicts and live at peace with himself. Whether they—or, indeed, Buddhism in general—can be classed as "religions" in any further sense of the word is partly a matter of semantics and classification. But one thing is clear enough. Anything which *can* be classed without ambiguity as a "religion"—Judaism, Christianity, Islam, Hinduism—will always include an element of that tranquillising kind, while placing its primary emphasis elsewhere. One could put it the other way round. We Catholics say that a man sins when he turns his back on God—he endangers his immortal soul. But he also endangers his immediate well-being. Man is a naturally religious animal. Any attempt to live on a totally irreligious basis is going to generate stress or conflict within the individual, and this, in its turn, will probably do various kinds of damage to his body and bring him before long to the doctor's surgery.

God is not to be regarded as a low-cost tranquilliser. But the stress-related diseases are epidemic in our time, and a very large proportion of those who go to the doctor's surgery do so for ultimately psychological reasons—as, presumably, do all of those who visit the psychiatrist or the psychoanalyst. Add to these the very much larger number of people who seek relief from the burden and conflict of self by chemical means alone, and it then becomes very hard indeed to avoid a certain suspicion that modern man is more deeply and extensively at war with himself than his ancestors ever were.

He differs from them in another way too: his secular-humanist culture represents humanity's first major attempt to live without any religion at all.

Could there be a connection between these two facts?

*   *   *

On such lines, and merely for the sake of human happiness, one would wish Europe's future to be deeply religious.

If given any primacy, of course, these pragmatic and psychological considerations will prove grossly insufficient and, in practice, self-destructive. Any religion which was pursued primarily for its tranquillising side-benefits would be pursued in a self-centred manner and therefore falsely—it would amount to little more than a camouflaged ego-trip. An honest man concerns himself primarily with the truth, and therefore with the seeking of God, rather than with his own immediate well-being of body or of mind. If inward peace then comes to him, it comes as a kind of by-product or bonus. And it seems to me that while religions differ profoundly and most crucially in their notions of God and man and of the relationship between the two, they do not differ very much in their ability to provide that side-benefit of inward peace. Not long ago I met a Zen abbot and, soon afterwards, a Catholic and Benedictine abbot; and they struck me as being very similar men, psychologically speaking, and possessed of an almost identical inner tranquillity. Comparable resemblances can be observed elsewhere. But it would be a disastrous mistake, in my view, to say that because all monasticisms and all religions can generate very much the same kind of personal tranquillity, any choice between them is going to be a matter of indifference, of personal taste. Any such inference would ignore the distinction between by-products and primary objectives.

But in this chapter, I am concerned with those pragmatical and psychological considerations alone; and despite the resemblances just mentioned, I suggest that the Benedictine monk has certain distinctive things to tell modern Europe about the individual's achievement of peace with himself.

But first, a certain ambiguity is to be noted; it arises from our tendency to understand the word "peace," too simply, as an absence of all conflict.

When you meet a monk, he will usually (not always) strike you as being indeed suffused with a most enviable kind of inner serenity and joy. An English visitor once asked a French monk to comment upon his life:

> He paused a moment and said, "Have you ever been in love?"
> I said, "Yes."
> A large Fernandel smile spread across his face. "Eh bien," he said, "c'est exactement pareil."

But too idyllic an interpretation of that reply would be misleading. One does not need to be an extreme cynic to observe that the experience of being in love is not always one of ideal tranquillity. As the poets and dramatists remind us, it can be a prolonged torment, an agony; and the same can be true of the Christian's love affair with God, especially when this is taken with the monk's kind of seriousness and made into a life's work. The recent convert or the newly-repentant sinner will often find his spiritual life surprisingly sweet and easy. But as he makes progress in it, the sky will grow darker—he will find himself engaged in a "spiritual combat" of the most arduous kind, shattering and even nightmarish at times. Many writers have attempted to describe "the dark night of the soul," and they all concur in representing it as something very unpleasant indeed.

There is an ugly sense in which Oscar Wilde was right when he said: "The only way to get rid of a temptation is to yield to it." In the same way, any country can always secure peace, of a sort, by surrendering at once to any threatening enemy. But the monk's peace is not of that kind: he is in fact steadily at war, if not precisely with himself, then at least with the assertiveness and self-love of his own ego, and this means that his life is one of sustained conflict.

How then can it also be a life of inner peace?

There is a certain sense in which "peace" and "conflict" can co-exist and even be friends, in joint antithesis to the soul-destroying kind of stress which stems from the avoidance or postponement of all conflict. This seeming paradox is borne out by our common experience in connection with actual war. In the summer and early autumn of 1939, for example, we in England—and, of course, others in other countries—felt a mounting pressure of apprehension and uncertainty. Was there going to be a war? It was an agonising question, tending to shatter any inward peace that we might otherwise have enjoyed. The actual declaration of war, when it came, released us from that pressure—it gave us a tremendous feeling of relief and release, and therefore, however paradoxically, of peace.

The front-line soldier commonly reports a similar experience. Before the battle is joined, he feels paralysed and unmade by suspense and fear. But throughout the actual fighting, he feels wonderfully detached and serene.

These analogies may cast some light upon the experience and psychology of that "happy warrior," the monk. He has engaged himself deeply in a conflict which most of us prefer to ignore or avoid or postpone. We thereby prolong in our own lives a particularly fruitless and destructive kind of pre-war or pre-battle stress, from which the monk is joyously free. He bases his life upon the acceptance of suffering and the elimination of anxiety, whereas we are made desperately anxious by our wholly negative attitude towards any kind of stress or conflict or pain. His model is Christ, the King who reigned most victoriously from the cross.

His happiness, his inner serenity is a very real thing. But let us not forget its dialectical nature and its high personal cost.

* * *

Even at our less heroic level, however, we can promote our own inner peace by attending to the message and model which he puts before us; and I intend no frivolity by defining this, initially, in musical terms.

Not long ago, I saw a television programme which was called simply "The Chant." It was a musical programme rather than a religious one; and while Plainsong or Gregorian Chant is the common property of the Western Church, it is the Benedictine monks' property in a special way, their great activity and *expertise*, so that this programme naturally took us into various cloisters and abbey churches. (It took us elsewhere as well; and I was glad to hear of the many clubs and choirs—including some of schoolchildren—which are learning and practising the Chant on a private basis, from motives which range from the purely musical and aesthetic to the purely religious.)

There were various comments, and I was particularly struck by two things which were said by an extremely intelligent lady—one who introduced herself, with imperfect plausibility, as an atheist. In the first place, she described Plainsong as the most effective tranquilliser one could possibly imagine. In saying this, she was not comparing it with some drug that dulls and stupefies. She was referring to its immense power to calm the inner turmoil of the mind and fill the hearer with peace. In the second place, she mentioned her reluctance to hear very much of it. She felt that it seriously endangered her atheism.

I think she was realistic in both respects. Many people have found that a spiritual retreat—within some monastery and, for a short time, under its discipline—offers a most useful healing of wounds and recharging of batteries. In a more immediate sense, and with no strictly religious question arising at all, a man tormented by inner conflict will always do well to go to some abbey like the one I had in mind when I wrote the first paragraphs of this book, and just sit quietly at the back of the church throughout the whole slow, chaste splendour of, say, Solemn Vespers, with his body at ease and his eyes shut and his ears open. He will find the experience a profoundly healing and reviving one. But he must not stay too long if, like that lady, he wishes to retain his atheism intact. The Chant silences the buzzing nonsense of the fretful mind and so brings peace. But it shows a particular tendency to silence the particular buzz of self-deception and self-assertion which we call "atheism" in one man and "sin" in another. It works almost sacramentally, signifying holiness while also helping to effect it within the hearer. It is a most powerful medicine for the feverish sick soul.

To me at least, its efficaciousness in this sense is something of a mystery; and all the more so, since Plainsong was never designed as a tranquilliser. Together with the liturgy of which it is the vehicle, it constitutes a highly-developed and finely-honed technique for doing one particular thing, of little direct relevance to the individual's psychological state—namely, the public and ordered worshipping of God. It is not the only way of doing this particular thing, but it is a supremely good way. Its benefits to the individual come as a kind of by-product.

Those interested in the psychology of music will perhaps see its efficacy, in this latter respect, in primarily rhythmical terms. Every army knows that when you want to turn men from peace to conflict, the insistent aggressive beat of the drums is going to be useful: loud violent regular rhythms can be hypnotic in effect, disposing the hearers towards mindless violence and—in certain circumstances—towards mindless sex as well. Hence the frenzy and also the eroticism of Pop or Rock music, which is undoubtedly the dominant art-form of today's secular world, just as Plainsong is the dominant art-form of the monks. Between the two, the contrast is total. The one expresses and also enhances feelings of agitation and aggression and inner turmoil: it is a social ritual of psychological violence and loveless eroticism, intended (as they say) to "blow the mind" into mindlessness, analogous to the cult of drug-taking and the strictly narcotic use of sex, and closely associated with those two things in practice. The other expresses and also enhances an inward chaste serenity of the mind, a peaceful enlargement of the spirit; and to some extent at least, it seems to do so by its careful *avoidance* of anything like a regular rhythm or beat, such as might be orgiastic in tendency on however small a scale. It has no such rhythm or beat; it has no time-signature at all, but flows in gentle irregularity like a cool river, speaking of peace, soothing the mind, opening the heart to God.

To contrast Plainsong with Pop or Rock is to contrast two extremes, and intermediate positions are clearly tenable: the musical time-signature, as such, is no instrument of Satan. But if we are concerned for the future of Europe, and

therefore for the inward peace of its people, we do need to
have some sort of concern for its music, the history of which
suggests that we took a fatally wrong turning at some point.
Plainsong was a powerfully formative influence upon its
first beginnings (this fact was clearly and beautifully
illustrated in a series of radio programmes called *Plainsong
and the Rise of European Music*, compiled by Basil Lam and
broadcast by the BBC in 1978), and there was a long
subsequent period—up to the time of Mozart, Schubert, and
early Beethoven—during which it still spoke of order, of
decorum, of tranquillity. But then came the romantic and
revolutionary period, and it suddenly began to speak of
agitation and turmoil and self-pity instead; and then came
Wagner, foreshadowing the spirit of Nazism—a spirit
which now expresses itself, even more clearly, in the
perverse eroticism and aggressive jackboot stamp of Rock.
And there is little comfort to be gained by turning to the
more "serious" music of our time, since this seems to be
mostly a negative thing, speaking only of chaos and
disintegration and meaninglessness.

There is more to this story than any mere pattern of
changing aesthetic preference. Music is a powerful thing. It
"has charms to soothe a savage breast," certainly; but in
suitable versions it can also inflame the peaceful breast into
savagery, or shatter the mind altogether. Change the music
of a nation, said Plato, and you'll find before long that you've
changed its laws—its society, its quality, its purpose. The
nature of Europe's future is going to depend, to some extent
at least, upon the nature of its dominant music.

I am not suggesting that Plainsong is the only tolerable
music. As I have observed, it is a specialised tool, a thing for
worshipping God with. None the less, if you want Europe to
be at peace, and if you therefore want its individual people to
be at peace with themselves, the monks offer you a good

model in this respect and a highly practical lesson. Sit there at the back of the abbey church through Solemn Vespers, and then go, for contrast, to some thunderous sweaty sexy *discothèque*. So far as Europe's future and peace is concerned, you will then have visited a crucial region where the roads fork.

*   *   *

In speaking of this contrast, I have made analogous use of the adjective "chaste" on the one side and the noun "eroticism" on the other. The analogy is not altogether an arbitrary one. Music affects us at the very centre of our being, and we didn't need Dr. Freud to tell us that the same is true of our sexuality.

And so, by a natural transition, we can turn now to a further sense in which the monk offers us a useful lesson in the matter of the individual's inward peace.

In the popular mind, the monk's celibacy is the most characteristic thing about him. When some man is said to "live like a monk," this commonly means that he lives chastely; and this is a curious usage, since the monk's celibacy is shared by all Catholic priests and by any number of unmarried Christian layfolk. But it makes a kind of sense. The monk is not merely a man who refrains from marriage and also—naturally, though not always easily—from those various sexual sins which are open to the unmarried. He aims higher than that. Among other things, he is called to a total, positive chastity of the body, the mind, the imagination.

The prevailing outlook of our time is such that the mere mention of such an ideal is likely to elicit a twofold response, of scepticism and also of disapproval. In the first place, it is widely believed that for a normal and healthy young man, any total discipline of the sexuality is—for all practical purposes—impossible. This assumption runs through all the familiar arguments about contraception, abortion, "family planning," "population control," and the like. Almost universally outside the Catholic Church—and here and there within it—people take it for granted that men and women, and schoolchildren as well, are wholly at the mercy of their sexual urges, so that abstinence or self-control is simply not a realistic option. There have been many influential thinkers (Malthus and Gandhi among them) who have thought otherwise without being Catholics at all. But in general, modern man seems to assume that while he has unlimited powers of the technological kind and can conquer and control Nature as he chooses, he has no power at all of the moral kind and cannot possibly be asked to conquer and control himself—especially in matters of sex.

Accordingly, sly cynical jokes are made about monastic celibacy, and not only by foolish or nasty-minded people. The monks cannot *really* be as celibate as is claimed! They must have their secret outlets, their indulgences, their gratifications, as suggested in the anecdotes of Boccaccio; and if these do not take the normal pattern of male eroticism, then of course the cloister must be a hotbed of secret homosexuality.

One great practical lesson, taught to us by the monks, is to the effect that any such assumption is gratuitous and false. Nobody supposes that chastity is an easy thing for the healthy male, or that total perfection—in this respect as in others—is going to be achieved very widely in this life; and it is certainly true that where monastic dedication and discipline starts to break down, as it occasionally does, chastity will be among the first things to go. To that extent, Boccaccio's picture of the monk can be a true one.

But it will be true exceptionally, not characteristically. Any close familiarity with Benedictine monasticism as it actually exists will provide ample evidence that the cynic is mostly wrong—that in this environment at least (and, a Catholic will add, by the grace of God), a perfectly normal and healthy man can in fact lead a chaste and celibate life, and that a great many such men do so on a day-to-day basis, from their first entering into the monastery until death. Contrary to what the modern world seems to believe, the thing can be done.

It can be done, moreover, without stress. Many people, while conceding that chastity is possible, look upon it with disapproval: it is an unnatural thing, a crippling, a distortion, a frustration, such as can only generate neurosis. The monk is therefore bound to be a nervous, tensed-up, bitter kind of man; human nature was not designed for his kind of life. But he seldom turns out to be like that in fact.

The assumption that he must inevitably do so is a widespread and very curious one. To some degree, it probably stems from popular misunderstandings of certain technical terms of psychoanalysis, notably "inhibition" and "repression"—as though any kind of self-control was going to be psychologically destructive. Freud knew better and intended nothing of that kind by his use of those words. More generally, a great many people seem to believe that if we are looking for peace of mind, for fulfilment and serenity, for happiness, our best hopes will lie in the immediate satisfaction of every felt desire, and every sexual desire in particular.

This is an extraordinary idea. It has no basis in psychology, and the wise men of every religion have agreed about its total and cruelly deceptive falsity, to which the actual workings-out of sexual "permissiveness," in our time, bear ample witness. It also represents a quite unworkable ideal. The actual needs of a human being are few in number and can be met fairly easily; but his possible desires—including those of the sexual kind—are boundless and cannot ever find total satisfaction. Those who seek their total satisfaction are doomed to seek forever; and for such people, sex—a good thing, designed by God for his own good purposes—will become an obsession and a torment.

In my capacity as a critic, I have to read a great many novels of the outspoken modern kind; and their writers—reporting truthfully, as a novelist must, upon the actual experience of people in society—are fairly unanimous (though often reluctantly so) in saying that sex becomes exactly that, an obsession and torment, when treated "permissively." They write, of course, from many different angles, and are not always aware of what they are saying. But their overall witness is clear, and it is backed up by the experience of every doctor, every psychiatrist, every social worker, and all too many parents of broken girls. The immediate indulgence of every desire does *not* make for serenity or inner peace.

In this respect as in others, the monk's inner peace is that of the "happy warrior" rather than of the pacifist. But it is perfectly genuine none the less, and not least in this important matter of sex. He does not simply reject or deny his own sexuality. He chooses to do something positive with it, as befits a possession of such inherent goodness and high personal value; and he therefore lays it up upon God's altar, in very much the spirit of those who once took care that the lamb sacrificed to God was perfect and without blemish, the best of the flock.

Such a decision is far from making this side of his life automatically easy. But then, the alternative good thing that he might have chosen to do with his sexuality—by offering or sacrificing it to some loved woman in marriage—would not have been altogether easy either.

The sexual obsession of our time is such that many people

talk as though celibacy was primarily, or even only, a matter of physical frustration. It imposes a further burden as well, and, as a man gets older, a heavier one: the celibate has to live without the pleasures of parenthood, and also without the support and strength of family life. The monk does, however, enjoy one comfort and relief which is not shared by the secular priest or by a large proportion of other celibates. He certainly has to do without the pleasures of parenthood. (In my experience, this fact makes him appreciate children very much, and they usually respond warmly.) But he does at least live within a *familia*, and with the psychological support which this fact gives. The accidents of his work may sometimes take him far afield—he may be something of a world-traveller. But when the time comes for him to grow old and die, he is not pensioned off into some home or institution, as an old horse is put out to grass. Some such destiny is the final burden and penance of many a parish priest. But the monk always has somewhere to go back to, a place where he belongs. He dies in the family home.

*　　*　　*

His whole approach to the questions of sex and love and home and family is one that offers much to the troubled mind of the modern European. But he offers us a further message of inward peace; and this concerns the importance and wisdom of attending to the present moment and to eternity, rather than to whatever is promised or threatened by the temporal future. He is not future-oriented; and this is one prime reason for his freedom from anxiety.

A careful distinction needs to be drawn here. In a certain sense, the Christian is future-oriented by the mere fact of his baptism and faith. He is almost defined by the fact that he awaits the blessed hope, the second coming of his Lord in glory.

But this fact is not quite what it seems. We live in space

and time, and our thought-forms and languages are shaped accordingly. While Einstein may have given some help to our imaginations, we still find it hard to think and harder still to talk outside our own familiar spatio-temporal framework. So long as we remember this limitation and our subjection to it, and are therefore suitably careful in our understanding and use of theological language, this does not matter so very much. But dangers still remain, and one of them is the danger of talking as though eternity meant a further (but now unlimited) supply of temporal duration, or as though the Kingdom was to reach its *pleroma* or consummation *within* the historical process, so that we can wisely and properly be future-oriented in some simply literal sense.

That is the illusion of the Marxists, and of those imprudent Christians who flirt with Marxist notions of history and salvation. The actual Coming will take us out of the historical process altogether: the actual Kingdom is not of this world—this *saeculum*, this spatio-temporal framework—anymore than Heaven is a "place" to which we might simply travel by our own initiative, if only we had a sufficiently powerful space rocket and the right navigational charts. Our final lift-off will be into a dimension that we cannot now imagine, even with Einstein's help.

The wise Christian, therefore, is only future-oriented in a qualified and distinctly limited sense. The virtue of prudence obliges him to take such care for his own future as is possible and appropriate; the virtue of charity obliges him to do the same for his neighbour's future. But having done what he can, he leaves the outcome to God and turns his attention back to the present moment, the point at which time touches eternity. He does not allow himself any tense emotional involvement in the various possibilities of good and evil that await him, or mankind in general, in this life.

This is one of the things that distinguish him from non-Christian man in general, and from the non-Christian people of this present age in an exceptional way. Humanity has always been future-oriented in some degree, as Pope observed:

Hope springs eternal in the human breast;
Man never is, but always to be blest.

But ever since the romantic and revolutionary period began at the end of the eighteenth century, ideas of "Progress" and "Evolution" have come to dominate the psychology of Europe and the West to a remarkable extent, causing men to place a high value upon change as such and, hence, to live more and more for expected future good, less and less for immediate present good. It thus came about that such adversative words as "stagnation" could be applied almost automatically to anything like the "stability" recommended by St. Benedict, vowed by his monks, and enjoyed over long periods in many secular societies. In recent years, this cult of change and the future seems to have lost much of its optimism. Where we once heard confident claims being made for "Progress," we now hear alarming prophecies of doom. But in this less cheerful version, the habit of future-orientation seems as powerful as ever it was.

I take it to be a bad habit, and for several reasons. For one thing, while we can make plausible guesses about the future, we cannot *know* anything about it, and can only determine its pattern in a very limited way. To fix our attention upon it is to turn away from reality. Then, the future is a lost cause. Every passing year, every passing day means that there is less and less of it, more and more of the past. All hopes for the temporal future come squarely up against the fact of death—the individual's death, and then that of our whole species—and must somehow compete with the existential dread which that fact must generate where it is faced honestly. And finally, any kind of future-orientation must always be the direct enemy of human happiness in the measure of its intensity, since it derives its entire dynamic from dissatisfaction with the present.

This last point is conspicuously true of the two great future-oriented ideologies which now compete for the soul of Europe. Consumer-capitalism promotes dissatisfaction with the present in a very straightforward way. Its entire market-system depends upon people always wanting more than they already have, and would be threatened most dangerously by any sudden outbreak of contentment. Communism achieves the same result in two different ways. Before the Revolution, while the Party is still in opposition, it does everything possible to inflame discontent and indignation. It tells people to make the most of their grievances, and not on any account to be happy with things as they are. (The trade-union baron, under capitalism, does exactly the same thing. His immense power depends upon the real or simulated discontents of his membership.) Then, when the Communist Party is in power, it hardly bothers to suggest that men ought to be *contented* with the fear, oppression, poverty, and general misery which it inflicts upon them. It calls upon them to endure, justifying those present evils (under various euphemistic names) by the promise of a golden millennium, to be attained at some unspecified time in the future.

Each of these two ideologies is therefore a direct enemy of contentment in the Now, which is the prime road to inner peace. In general, we can say that future-orientation makes for anxiety and stress, while attention to the present moment and to eternity is the path of relaxation and wisdom.

This is a path along which Europe might usefully follow the monk. He is not future-oriented. He has chosen a life in which—ideally at least—he simply isn't going to *have* any temporal future, such as might differ from his present and his past and so give him scope for ambition and anxiety. In practice, his life usually does include at least some possibility of change. He may become abbot one day, he may be given some other particular office within the community, he may be among those who go forth like swarming bees to establish a daughter-community elsewhere. But all such possibilities are anomalous, exceptional, alien to his vocation as a monk, deserving little of his attention and no concern or anxiety at all. He is called to changelessness, to an ordering of his mind around the expectation that until he dies, each day or week or year is going to resemble the previous one, allowing only for the steady cycle of the liturgical year. "Rien ne change dans la vie monastique," said one abbot to his novices. "Chaque jour est pareil à l'autre, chaque année comme celle qui la précédait, et ainsi jusqu'à la mort."

Such timelessness, such repose in the Now and in eternity, is unlikely to characterise the actual daily lives of ordinary men outside the cloister. But we could all bring something of its spirit into our lives; and in so far as Europe managed to do so, it would achieve a most important kind of peace, while also putting a great many psychiatrists out of business and dealing a mortal blow to the tranquilliser industry.

Certain economic problems might then arise. But why worry? If the Christian has been told anything at all, he has been told not to become anxious about economic problems.

*   *   *

Such contentment in the present is not always and automatically an easy thing to achieve. Its difficulty seems to be a matter of outlook and temperament, rather than of circumstances. Adversity, especially when shared, can sometimes turn out to be its unexpected ally. The seemingly fortunate are often the discontented, the shrill, the bitter, the violent. At the time of writing, the most conspicuous challenges to Europe's peace are those offered by terrorism in various versions, and it has often been observed that the people concerned are, characteristically, the children of wealthy and comfortable homes.

The answer to the problem of contentment, or inward peace of mind, is not economic in nature or otherwise simple. But there is one central and indeed simple key to it, and the monks put their collective finger upon this a long time ago.

You wake up every morning, and you emerge from the confusion of dreams, and the problems and the business of life start to rush in upon your reluctant consciousness. What are those problems? What is the business of life? As a man of the world, you will probably answer such questions in some more or less complicated fashion. But if you wake up in a monastery, you will be reminded at once that they are essentially simple. What wakes you up is not a bell, but a knock on the door and a pair of quietly uttered words which amount to an exhortation and even an order: *Benedicamus Domino*, "let us praise, or bless, or thank the Lord." Your proper reply is an indication that you have in fact woken up, but is also an act of obedience to that command: *Deo gratias*, "Thanks be to God." You start the monastic day by an expression of gratitude.

It is the duty of all men to praise and thank their Creator, but it is the monk's task in a special way; and if each monk is at peace with himself, this is largely because he lives gratefully. That is why his life, although austere, is traditionally led in surroundings of some beauty. The goodness of the Creator would be no less present in ugly surroundings, but it would be less *obviously* present, and the task of gratitude would then be more difficult. I remember one early morning in a Dutch abbey when I was awakened by those words of command and obeyed with my *Deo gratias*, and then went to the window and gazed out upon the misty green of a September dawn, which hares and squirrels were celebrating riotously among the bushes and across the dewy grass, while the pale autumnal sun rose silently. It was easy, then, to join in with those animals' sub-rational office of Lauds and thank the Lord. It would have been less easy (though no less obligatory) if I had woken up in some noisy and polluted atmosphere and stepped across to a window which looked out upon urban decay and industrial squalor.

Musically and architecturally too, as well as in various higher senses, the monk leads a life which conduces to an inner ordering and tranquillity of the mind, and therefore to a grateful awareness of the goodness which resides in *all* being, and not merely in human experience of the affluent and otherwise fortunate kind. His attitude to life is symbolised by the fact that he and his brethren sing a very long Latin grace together before sitting down to a distinctly simple meal, and another when they rise up afterwards; whereas it is the world's instinct to demand as lavish a meal as circumstances permit, and to express no gratitude at all for the pleasure and support which it gives.

With the moral and theological implications of this sharp contrast, I am not here concerned. My present point is that as a matter of empirical observation and experience, the monk's outlook and way of life makes for contentment and peace of mind, whereas the spirit of greed and envy and grievance—which is so conspicuously active in the present-day West—makes for inward stress, tension, bitterness, ulcers, and (all too frequently) mental breakdown.

At this inward and individual level also, Europe needs a little of St. Benedict's wisdom. Each one of us knows, or should know, that his own assertive ego needs to be fought and killed, and that this may involve a lifetime of hard campaigning. In that particular sense, inward peace is unattainable in this life. But in what further sense is there any point at all in being at war with yourself? You can't win. Any possible victory means that you've lost the fight.

Shalom, say the monks, *pax*: abandon that silly conflict. And as a prime means of doing so, live gratefully.

CHAPTER SIX

I n the cities of today, *graffiti* have come to abound. Their content is often highly objectionable, but they sometimes say good things. Close to where I live, for example, somebody has adorned a blank brick wall with a simple message in large white-painted letters: GET RIGHT WITH GOD. The wall in question is close to the railway station, and I often find myself contemplating those words while waiting for a train.

They offer us a useful message indeed; and it is also the message primarily offered to us by the monk, whose life is not primarily ordered towards the untying of psychological knots, or the resolution of social and political conflicts, or the establishment of an ecologically sound life style. Peace with oneself, peace with one's fellow-men, peace with the non-human creation that we see around us—all these are excellent and most desirable things, and we would like them to characterise the life of our European future as fully as possible. But the monk is not concerned with such things except in the most secondary and indirect way. Above all else, he calls upon us to make our peace with God. We are born in a state of alienation from God, and even at war with him. He comes and makes his peace with us at Baptism, but thereafter—whenever we sin, whenever we turn our backs upon him—we behave like treacherous rebels who go through the motions of submission but then continue the fight, which is very ungrateful of us. Our prime and almost our *only* duty, therefore, is that of laying down our arms and accepting peace with him and on his terms—a kind of peace which the world cannot give or even understand. It is to this purpose that the monk's life, of prayer and ordered worship and spiritual reading and penance and obedience and work, is primarily ordered; and it is in this respect, above all, that you and I and the whole of Europe must get his message and follow his example as far as circumstances permit.

I have not the faintest desire to play down this message: I regard its primacy as absolute, and I honour whatever man it was who wrote those words on that brick wall almost as I honour the monk. But my purpose in this book has been that of supplementing and reinforcing it with certain secondary considerations. If we all lived a bit more like monks and "got right with God," we would serve God better and move more swiftly and certainly towards our eternal rendezvous with him. Ideally speaking, that motivation ought to be enough for anybody. But in the weak and muddled creatures that most of us are, it does not always operate as powerfully as it should; and it therefore needs to be helped along by the secondary motivations provided by my principal theme—the fact that if we all lived a bit more like monks, a great many of our temporal problems would ease themselves automatically, to a considerable degree at least, giving us various kinds of temporal peace where we now appear to be stuck forever with stress and conflict.

An apparent paradox arises here. The monastic values and virtues may indeed help us to be at peace with God. But how can they possibly do anything for our civilisation and our temporal well-being? Their whole basis and starting-point is a firm rejection of all such considerations. Monasticism was never an attempt to "save civilisation." Very much the reverse. Its first beginnings, in the African desert, were a flat rejection of everything that the word "civilisation" then implied; and throughout its later development—especially in bloody and anarchic times—it always included an element of despair, so far as temporal well-being was concerned. That famous monk, St. Gregory the Great, for example,

> who was certainly not lacking in a sense of social responsibility, deliberately dissuaded his friends from entering the public service on the ground that the world was nearing its end and that it was better to seek the peace of the cloister, in which a man becomes already a partaker in eternity, than to become involved in the temporal anxieties and ambitions that are inseparable from the service of the state.

From such an outlook and scale of values, from so radical a writing-off of this world, how can we expect any but the most purely spiritual and other-worldly kind of good to emerge?

Yet St. Gregory the Great has to be listed among history's great civilisers; and the same is true of St. Benedict and of the monastic institution in general, as I observed in the first chapter of this book.

If the apparent paradox causes us any trouble or bewilderment, this may be partly because we live in a very technological society and therefore tend to see all things— rather too simply—in terms of cause and effect, of problem and solution, of effort and success. We know that men's exertions often fail or succeed imperfectly. But in so far as they succeed at all, we expect them to achieve something more or less like their directly intended purpose. We certainly do not expect them to achieve any purpose upon which the people concerned have firmly and deliberately turned their backs. Imagine, for example, that there's talk of bridging some river. The engineers study the matter and agree that the task simply cannot be done with the available resources; and it turns out, upon enquiry and discussion, that nobody really wants this bridge at all. So the project is dropped altogether, and by unanimous agreement. It is decided to devote the resources in question to building a sports pavilion instead. We shall then expect to see a sports pavilion in due course, and it may or may not be a good one. But we shall be extremely surprised if the bridge also comes mysteriously into existence.

But comparable things do happen in less technological areas. We often need to aim off target, and achieve some result most successfully by forgetting all about it. Health and happiness provide us with obvious examples. Health is a plainly desirable thing; but if we take our health too seriously and make it the object of our constant concern, we shall probably worry ourselves sick and become hypochondriacs. So with happiness. This is a moral duty in one sense, a piece of uncovenanted good fortune in another. If we try to secure it for ourselves, by effort and contrivance, we shall only make ourselves anxious and miserable. Thomas Jefferson made life much more difficult for the Americans when he told them—in their most sacred document—that happiness is something which can be *pursued*. It is not.

This seeming paradox is in fact a familiar fact of human psychology, and of spirituality as well. It runs all through the Gospel. He who saves his life shall lose it; and in the same way, those who set out to establish a Utopia of worldly peace commonly succeed in establishing a worldly Hell. The important thing is to make our peace with God and seek his other-worldly Kingdom. In so far as temporal well-being is available at all in this life—it certainly eludes us when pursued directly—it will then come to us as a kind of by-product.

The matter could be stated in stronger terms. The pursuit of temporal well-being, directly and without reference to our prior need to be at peace with God, shows a marked tendency to prove not only difficult but self-defeating. It might be assumed that temporal peace, of the three kinds which I have been discussing, is such an obviously desirable thing as to make *any* pursuit of it inherently innocent and praiseworthy, with or without any further reference to God. But such an assumption would be rash. Any pursuit of temporal peace, if not related from the start to God and his law, is going to be radically tainted, and is therefore likely to display some very ugly features before long and so promote further conflict and other kinds of disaster.

Anyone who faces the manifest fact of original sin will perceive the inherent probability of this. But concrete experience tells us the same story. Take, for example, the pursuit of peace and harmony as between man and Nature, the non-human world around us. This has led to the environmental and "ecological" movement of the present time, which is an admirable thing in itself. In much of our recent past, we have treated God's world altogether too aggressively, too greedily, too violently, as though "Nature" was no mother but rather an enemy, to be beaten down and exploited. Many people have now come to see the impiety and folly of this, and have said various wise things about pollution, and the waste of non-renewable resources, and the dangers created by technomania and the worship of economic growth. So far, so good. But then—*normally*, not just in exceptional cases—they go on from that point to speak of "over-population,"a concept which only makes sense on Manichaean or totalitarian premises; and with that supposed danger in mind, they propose the wholesale perversion of human sexuality, the forcible mutilation of the poor, and a Nazi-type "final solution" for the problems sometimes presented by the unborn child—all in the name of "respect for life"!

In the same way, the search for peace as between one man or one nation and another is a less simply innocent thing than it may appear. Unless related from the start to God and his law, it leads straight to the Secret Police, the Lubyanka prison, and the Gulag Archipelago. We should never forget for a moment that Communism started off as a *good* idea, and is still regarded as a good idea by many people whose hearts are innocent and whose motivations are praiseworthy, however defective in common sense and historical realism they may be. To lay aside religion as being altogether too uncertain and divisive; to join in brotherhood instead of competing; to share things in friendship instead of grabbing them selfishly; to eliminate the sufferings of the poor and the arrogance of the rich as well—it sounds so obvious a wisdom, so promising a road to peace! Yet whenever the experiment has been tried on a Marxist or otherwise materialistic basis, the outcome has been a more or less brutal tyranny, a country run like a prison-camp, in which the citizen is surrounded by barbed wire and does not dare to raise his voice.

It must always be so. The search for peace as between man and man, without reference to God, does not abolish violence. It merely makes violence—like so much else—into a big State monopoly.

Finally, the desire to live at peace with oneself—if pursued for its own sake—tends naturally to become just another form of self-seeking and self-indulgence, a Stoic or Buddhist *apatheia*, an indifference to all things. Alternatively, it can find a kind of satisfaction at a grossly animal level: a drunk, snoring and belching in the gutter, is wonderfully at peace with himself. Internal conflict stems partly from our awareness of the difference between what we are and what we should be; and we can always relieve it, in a way, by ceasing to think about what we should be and wallowing in the existential reality of what we are: "Simply the thing I am shall make me live."

Inward serenity of the ascetic but proud and self-centred kind is a nihilistic thing and offers little for Europe's future. Mere "permissiveness" is uglier still and offers less. The monk, with his primary emphasis upon peace with God, is a much more practical man.

*   *   *

If we are to make practical use of his wisdom, in this ultimate matter, certain widely-cherished presumptions of present-day secular thinking will need to be called seriously in question. In particular, we shall need to say that "the religious question"—if I may so describe it—is of primary and public importance, and not merely a matter of the individual's private hunches and preferences. We shall also need to say that it is not doomed to remain a question for ever, a scepticism, an agnosticism. It is in fact capable of definitive solution.

Each of these two principles will arouse sharp opposition in some quarters. None the less, each is of the greatest practical importance for our future, as well as being necessary in principle. Peace with God comes first, say the monks. Translated into the language of daily affairs, this means that the religious question comes first, being logically, *and in practice*, anterior to every major question of the social or political, or economic or educational kind. We can ignore this fact, but we cannot evade its consequences. Europe's future depends upon what we do, and this in turn depends upon what we believe. Any action that we take, in the world of practical affairs, involves *some* kind of prior presumption about what human beings are, and what they are for, and what ultimate destiny faces them, and what rights and duties they have, and from what natural or supernatural source they derive these. Radical disagreement about such matters makes for social incoherence and breakdown—for anarchy on the one hand or the equal "disorder" of tyranny on the other. It eliminates any possibility of order, and therefore of peace, as the present state of the West shows clearly enough.

If Europe is to have any future as a peaceful community, the first thing it needs is a faith in common, believed by the great majority if not by all, forcibly imposed upon nobody but embodied in its public institutions and serving as the basis of its law and policy. I take this to be a necessity of the simply pragmatic sort, an anthropological fact about the behaviour of human beings in society, however deeply it may offend those who make toleration and therefore pluralism into absolute values. If the monks live together at peace, this is partly because they share a common faith.

But it is not enough for Europe to have *some kind* of faith in common. It needs not merely "religion" in the abstract but religious truth, and, once again, for reasons that are partly pragmatic. Illusion is always deleterious in the long run, though it sometimes offers brief comfort. If any action is based upon erroneous premises, its outcome is (in general) likely to be less satisfactory than it would have been if based upon true premises. Universally-shared delusions might make for social cohesion in some degree, but could hardly provide any sound basis for practical action; and even if they did, only an extreme cynic would desire them to prevail.

If the monks live together at peace, this is not only because they share a common faith; it is also because they share the *true* Faith, so that their lives and minds are deeply rooted in reality. This is one part of what "living at peace with God" must necessarily mean, since "truth" is one of the names of God.

The dominant scepticism of our time, together with

certain popular understandings of "ecumenism," means that all such talk of a one-and-only "true Faith" is going to encounter sharp hostility, as being arrogant and divisive. Any such challenge will need to be faced squarely; and it is my impenitent view that the scepticism in question is a paralysis of the mind, makes for nihilism and despair, and is the most hateful and insidious of all the internal enemies which now confront the West. (I would add that unless certain distinctions are drawn very carefully, "ecumenism" becomes a comparable paralysis of the religious mind and is then the enemy of Christian unity, not its friend at all.)

If only for the sake of Europe's peace we must recover the lost art of positive thinking; and once we have broadened our minds a little and come to accept the possibility that there might actually *be* a one true Faith, the problem of identifying it will not be a difficult one. There is only one serious and plausible candidate, and it has the solid backing of the monks. The search for peace can start at a great many points. But if undertaken with rigour and realism, it will direct us unambiguously towards the faith and morals and worship and discipline of the Roman Catholic Church.

If we care about Europe's future, it must be our first desire that Europe should return to the Faith which made it—not as being historically and socially useful (though it is), but as being true. It is the appointed instrument of peace or reconciliation with God, and it is therefore the best possible road to those other and secondary kinds of peace.

*   *   *

This is not a work of apologetics, and I do not propose to offer here any general defence of this view. It is unfortunately necessary to add that I am here referring to the faith and morals and worship and discipline of the Roman Catholic Church as traditionally understood and as authoritatively set forth, and very definitely *not* to any of the various diluted Catholicisms and half-Catholicisms which have received so much publicity during these post-Conciliar years. Everything of that kind is an attempt to have it both ways, and can only confuse the issue.

But the monastic institution, considered in the broadest possible sense, does bear a kind of oblique historical witness to the rightness of the specifically Roman Catholic Faith, and precisely *because* it is not an exclusively Roman Catholic thing.

In all its versions, it is primarily a seeking of peace with God, or with a limited apprehension of God, and could never deserve any harsh words at all. I have spoken of the one true Faith, and I would wish that phrase to be understood in an uncompromisingly Roman Catholic sense. But I would wish to imply friendly rather than hostile things about Mount Athos and the whole tradition of Orthodox monasticism, and about the Benedictine monasticism which exists (on a very small scale) within the Church of England, and also about Buddhist and other non-Christian monasticisms in general. Within these frameworks a great many men have sought peace on lines more or less analogous to those followed by St. Benedict's Catholic monks, and fruitfully. The true Light enlightens every man born into this world; and while I attribute unqualified "truth" to one definable Faith, I suspect that it would be beyond the wit of man to devise a *totally* fallacious religion.

And yet, I find something significant in the fact that Benedictine and Catholic monasticism *works* much better than any other. I am not saying that those other monks have never succeeded in finding peace, or indeed God. But they have never had anything like the Benedictine impact upon history. If (like me) you want to argue that the monk is of primary importance as a maker and defender of civilisation—precisely *because* he makes nothing of that kind his primary concern—you have a strong case. But it only remains a strong case so long as you confine your attention to monasticism of the Benedictine and Catholic kind. The enormous historical impact of this was considered by Christopher Dawson, who then went on to say:

> No doubt...there have been other cultures—Tibet, Burma, and Ceylon, for example—in which a non-Christian monasticism played a somewhat similar role. But these were secondary or marginal cultures which have had little influence on the course of world history. The situation in China is more comparable, since there we have an example of a great world culture which was influenced by the coming of Buddhist monasticism at the very period when Western and Byzantine culture were being moulded by Christian monasticism. But, in China, the old tradition of Confucian learning remained intact and the Buddhist monks never took the place of the Confucian scholars. In the West, on the other hand, the educational institutions of the Roman Empire were swept away by the barbarian invasion or declined and died with the declining city culture of the Latin world. It was only by the Church and, particularly, by the monks that the tradition of classical culture and the writings of classical authors, "the Latin classics," were preserved.

There are more important matters than the preservation of ancient texts. But Dawson's general point remains a sound one. Monasticism, in the broadest sense of the word, is a retreat from the world and from history, a determination to have no impact upon the course of events. But when fertilised (so to speak) by the Catholic Faith, it suddenly blossoms out into something of extraordinary dynamism, but, paradoxically, without losing its original and very non-dynamic, non-assertive nature.

The key to this mystery is theological. What makes Benedictine monasticism so curiously effective in history, and so important therefore for the past and also (if we give it a chance) for the future of Europe, is its synthesis of the ascetic

or life-denying principle with the incarnational or life-
affirming principle; and this synthesis is only made possible
by that infinitely subtle balance or dialectic between the
flesh and the spirit, nature and supernature, Cross and
Resurrection, which we call "Catholicism."

There is a sense in which the opposite of the word
"Catholic" is something like "unbalanced" or "one-sided."
It is no easy thing to keep one's balance—to recognise the
goodness of this creation on the one hand, and the fact of evil
on the other; to entertain no foolish Pelagian or Panglossian
optimism about the human condition, while also avoiding
those denials and despairs which characterise Eastern
religion. Psychology and experience will always be tending
to throw us off balance, in the one direction or the other. The
thing which holds us to the narrow road of sanity is doctrine,
and history confirms the theological principle that doctrine
only retains its balanced or "Catholic" character in the
tradition and discipline of that Church which we define by
its unity with the See of Peter.

In that sense, the whole monastic phenomenon does point
unambiguously towards the specifically Roman Catholic
Faith. Without that Faith, it remains a limited and local
thing, a partially wise denial. But with that Faith—and, for
all practical purposes, with no other—it becomes a denial
which is also an affirmation, and which therefore resounds
through history.

*   *   *

It is the first business of mankind to be reconciled with
God, to know him and love him and serve him in this world
and be happy with him forever in the next. And as responsible Europeans, concerned for the future of our part of the
world, we have the prime duty of preaching the Catholic
Faith in its full integrity and so bringing men back to the

one appointed instrument of reconciliation with God in Christ.

There are many possible approaches to this task, and they have proved variously effective in the past. But as many of us know from bitter experience, "modern man" is quite exceptionally resistant to *any* process of evangelisation. When you put the Faith before him, he doesn't exactly deny its truth, as his robust nineteenth-century forefathers did. Instead, he denies its "relevance": he just isn't interested at all. He is very seldom a full-blooded dogmatic atheist. But his mind naturally works on lines which are Gnostic or Pelagian or both, and he has no sense of Original Sin. Seldom indeed does he see the problems of his condition in terms of a bad relationship—of alienation and conflict— between himself and God. So if you offer him peace or reconciliation with God, he takes no interest. Where the Gospel is concerned, he lacks "ears to hear."

Many Christians, including some Catholics, respond to this difficulty on lines which I take to be disastrous. They overlook the Lord's warning that the seeds of the Gospel would sometimes fall upon stony ground and be wasted. They are anxious to see results of *some* kind, and so they seek out seeds of some other and coarser kind, capable of germinating in that stony ground; and they are thus enabled to gather a thin harvest of weeds, which they proudly offer as a new and more relevant kind of wheat. The world refuses to listen to the traditional Gospel? Very well, then, let us find what the world *will* listen to, and call that the new or modernised Gospel, giving it just a top-dressing of Christian and Catholic terminology for the sake of plausibility. Then we shall get a hearing. The Church will seem relevant once again.

This does not in fact happen. The world has no particular reason for listening to a Church which only echoes its own concerns and values. But the outcome is not always totally weed-like. It is mostly a matter of increased concern for social welfare, and this is no bad cause when considered in psychological terms. Boredom and loneliness are among the great evils of our time, and a modernised pseudo-Christianity is one of the things that can ease them in some degree by offering an imaginative stimulus and human togetherness. But where social welfare is conceived in political and economic terms, any such "religion" has a notorious tendency to acquire a Marxist flavour before very long; and at its very best, it bears practically no resemblance to that "orient and immortal wheat" which gives us the Bread of Life.

It is an axiom of salesmanship that you have to start with the *present* problems and preoccupations of the prospective buyer—with what he supposes himself to want, rather than with what he really needs; which does not mean that you have to stop there. Those who understand this principle too simply may indeed gain something of the "relevance" which is their primary concern, but at the cost of their authentic Christianity.

In recommending St. Benedict as Europe's patron, I am proposing, among other things, an alternative and sounder way out of that same difficulty. It is certainly true that any evangelist must engage himself with people as he actually finds them; and it is equally true that in our time, he characteristically finds them unaware of being alienated from God and in conflict with him, and therefore deaf to any offer of reconciliation or peace with God.

But they are not totally deaf; and at the three temporal levels which I have been discussing in this book, they are sharply and anxiously aware of alienation and conflict, and are therefore likely to give sympathetic attention to any well-tested and practical peace-formula. They will probably dismiss the Catholic priest, as such, out of hand—he offers them nothing which they can recognise as relevant to their own problems. Initially, they may well be disposed to dismiss the monk in very much the same way, as an essentially negative and unimportant character. But with a little patient explanation, he can often be "sold" to them when Christ cannot. His "relevance" is not in fact greater, but it can often be more apparent. People's ears can then be opened to him more easily than to his Lord.

This fact can be illustrated by a small-scale social experiment. Suggest, in suitable company, that some secular problem might solve itself if we thought and behaved on more deeply Christian lines. You will commonly find yourself up against a solid brick wall of dismissive amusement. But substitute the word "monastic" for "deeply Christian," and you will find it much easier to get a sympathetic response. There may be initial mockery, but this will be much less confident and indestructible. It will often prove a wall of paper rather than of brick. And yet the monk's life is nothing more or less than the Christian life, led in community and in a particular style and dedication.

The point is that it offers visible success in a field dominated by failure. A great many thoughtful people of our time, although not consciously "religious" at all, are very much aware of our need to find some way of living together in brotherhood, at peace with the natural environment and with one another, at peace with ourselves as well. But they are also aware of the sad fact that our attempts to do so show a marked tendency to fail in one way or another. The hippie communes of the last few years were one such attempt, and they came to very little. Communism is another such attempt, and its outcome—although all too substantial—has been very unlovable indeed. One might even attribute the distinctive stresses of American life to the fact that the

United States was conceived from the start as a kind of Utopian community and not simply as just another country. As a country, it is no kind of failure. But it is no exception to the sad principle that Utopian communities disappoint those who put faith in them.

To modern Europe, St. Benedict offers history's greatest exception to that principle. A monastery is not exactly a Utopian community, and its inhabitants are not always perfect. Men seldom live up to their own best principles in any full, consistent, and lifelong pattern. They and their institutions go through good periods and bad periods, and while Benedictine monasticism has (by any human reckoning) a remarkably good record, it is no exception to this general rule. It has gone through some bad patches. Like the Catholic Church in general, it might be said to be going through a bad patch now. But in its values and ideals, and very considerably in its practice, an objective mind will recognise an outstandingly successful approach to the problem of wise living, a uniquely practical road to that threefold peace which all men seek, and therefore a model or pattern for the good life in general, quite apart from any religious considerations.

But the more thoughtful will then come to recognise the necessary basis of its practical success—the fact that it points beyond itself to the fourth and ultimate kind of peace, which only achieves complete fulfilment in Christ, and in the Faith and morals and life of his Church.

*   *   *

The monastic ideal is of such multiple and obvious relevance to the most urgent secular preoccupations of our time—on the lines which I have tried to indicate in this book—that it provides us with an exceptionally useful method or strategy for the Catholic apostolate. It is our prime task to help all men to become Christians, all Christians to become true Catholics, and all Catholics to become saints. It is a task which only grace can accomplish, but which we must forward to the best of our ability, using our prudential judgment as to the means that we can employ most usefully, the package—if I may use a vulgar commercial metaphor—which will help us most substantially to sell the Product. I have just been suggesting that to the men of this age (or a large proportion of them), the Christian and Catholic Product will be most easily sold if we give it St. Benedict's kind of packaging. It is in that primary sense that Europe needs St. Benedict for its patron.

But if I concluded on this note, I would suggest a more purely spiritual and apostolic purpose than has in fact prompted me to write this book. The practical wisdom of St. Benedict and his monks does indeed have its apostolic and apologetic usefulness: we can use it as a means of drawing men to peace with God in Christ and his Church, using their present and secular preoccupations as our starting-point. But we can also make a more immediate use of it. Those secular preoccupations are by no means unreal or unimportant in themselves, and while the Faith puts the primary emphasis elsewhere, it does not tell us to ignore them. Peace with God involves an active desire—expressed in the most central of our prayers—that his will should be actually implemented in this world and not only in Heaven. It therefore involves us in an active concern for this world as his property, made and loved by him, and a greater concern for our neighbours as the children for whom he died, and even a proper concern for ourselves. None of these things could matter very much if there were no God, and if this world and our life within it were only a meaningless accident of astronomical and evolutionary chance. But as things are, they matter a great deal.

Natural man, as such, has an instinct to care for the proper ordering of things in this life. But this is a weak and confused instinct, easily over-ridden by self-assertion and other passions and lusts, erratic in its operation, productive of some good but of much evil, too. The Faith gives us a new and powerful motivation for taking all such matters very seriously indeed, together with much sound guidance as to how we should handle them; and within the Faith, this is notably true of St. Benedict's Rule and spirit and the life led by his monks. If Europe needs him for its patron, this is also because it stands in rather desperate need of his distinctive and very practical wisdom in the mere conduct of its day-to-day life. The other-worldliness of this is precisely what makes it useful in and for this world.

Present-day Europe has all the cleverness one could desire—rather more than is good for it, perhaps—but seems rather short on wisdom. Many wise men certainly live within its boundaries. But collectively, as a community of peoples, it seems lost and uncertain, bewildered, technically and superficially "at peace" but profoundly divided and in a state of conflict with itself. The omens for its future are not encouraging.

As Europeans—and more so as Catholics, not less so—we should care about its temporal future; and my suggestion, in this book, is that we can do so most effectively by invoking the values of St. Benedict at every point of choice and decision, in matters great and small, in our own lives and—in so far as we have influence as rulers and parents and employers and writers and teachers and so forth—in the life of society as a whole.

We face many problems. I have classified them as being broadly environmental, social, and psychological—as concerning peace with the world around us, with one another, and with ourselves. Within each of these categories, we find that the problems in question have been solved by the monks as perfectly as they can ever be solved by men in this life, and that they can be solved by the rest of us—at least in some degree—in so far as we start to think and live a little more monastically.

In a Europe which had effectively made St. Benedict into its patron, we would live rather more simply, more modestly and gently than we now do, and with less of our present quasi-Marxist obsession with economics, our quasi-Manichaean obsession with technology and change. We would hear less noise and see more green; we would have less contention and more contentment; we would work rather harder and live rather longer, with fewer of us struck down in middle life by the diseases related to stress and anxiety. Our food might be simpler, but it would taste better; we might start, once again, to erect buildings worth looking at. Our social life—and our family life above all—would be stronger, more ordered, more structured, more organic; we might lose certain minor and questionable freedoms, while regaining the immensely supportive sense of belonging. There would be authority, there would be obedience; but there would be very little bullying and very little cringing, and not a great deal of politics. In so far as peace is attainable in this world, we would be at peace with ourselves, with each other, and with our natural environment. We might even be at peace with God.

Nothing is easier than idle dreaming about possible Utopias; and in order to forestall any criticism on those lines, I invoke the monks as hard evidence that such a life is no mere sentimental fantasy, no idyllic dream of Eden. It is certainly unlike the life which most of us live today, and very unlike the future towards which Europe is being impelled by the most conspicuous forces of the times. But it is not impossible. It is in fact entirely "natural," in the sense of being in accordance with human nature. And it is actually being lived—now, as you read these words—by any number of men, and of women too, who are of our own kind and not exceptional or heroic at all, but have chosen the Benedictine way. I have met them. I have tasted their peace.

It can be Europe's life as well, in so far as we choose that same way and follow it in some degree at least, according to our various circumstances.

How likely are we to do so? I cannot say. The future is a mystery, and cannot be predicted or controlled by ourselves except in the most limited way. My own cautious guesses are mostly pessimistic. I suspect that Europe faces a period of breakdown and disaster, during which—as during similar periods in its earlier days—the monastic institution will have a historical function rather like that of Noah's Ark when the floods came. A crucial function indeed! Let's hope that I'm wrong. But if I am, its historical function will be no less crucial—if we do not need it as an Ark, we shall still need it as a lighthouse or beacon, an aid to our navigation in this world.

> Monasticism has two things to offer to civilisation of the future: sanity and hope. By stressing the right order of values, monasticism, in a world of unbalance, stands for sanity. By keeping alive, in a world of mutual mistrust, an awareness of man's dignity and of his relationship in charity to the rest of the human race, monasticism brings with it hope.

Only a few of us can actually be monks, but any or all of us can decide to be guided by the monastic ideal and make our temporal decisions in the light which it provides. "The monastery is an essential dialectical fact in Christianity, and we need to have it there like a lighthouse, in order to gauge where we are—even though I myself should not exactly go into one." (That last qualification being my own no less than Kierkegaard's, and probably yours as well.) The cloister is a home for the few but a lighthouse or beacon for the many. It fights madness and despair by showing us that ordinary men can, after all, live sanely and wisely and peacefully in this world, and by demonstrating the straightforward though laborious art of doing so.

As Europe's patron, St. Benedict can help us substantially towards our ultimate destination, which is not of this world. But in the short term, he can help to make our voyage a great deal more serene and peaceful and appreciative, a great deal more appropriate therefore to the destiny and good fortune which makes us the inhabitants of so lovely and varied a continent, the inheritors of so rich a tradition.

Let his spirit guide our lives, and determine the decisions that we take in matters great and small. And if we ever feel lost and perplexed, exhausted by the tumult and stress which will characterise our life even then, we shall know where to turn for healing, for peace, for a recovery of values and direction. We shall only need to go back to that dark and chilly abbey church in which this book began, or to one like it, and sit in its quietly echoing holiness until the bell tolls once again and the monks come filing in to say their distinctive thing, addressed only to God but—for that reason—most beneficial to our immediate and worldly selves if we are wise enough to listen to it.

It begins with *Deus in adjutorium meum intende*, with the great human cry of suffering mankind in extremity, "God help me!" And it ends with the even deeper wisdom of *Deo gratias*, "Thanks be to God!"

Let us indeed give thanks to the Lord our God: *Vere dignum et justum est*, and Europe could act on no better principle.